CATNIP
OF LIFE

CATNIP
OF LIFE
poetry

Your gateway to understanding
Mother Nature's footprints by

SHARLA LEE

Copyright 2023 by Sharla Lee

All rights reserved. No part of this book may be reproduced or transmitted in any form or by any means without written permission of the publisher, except in the case of brief quotations embedded in critical articles and reviews.

This material has been written and published solely for educational purposes. The author and the publisher shall have neither liability nor responsibility to any person or entity with respect to any loss, damage, or injury caused or alleged to be caused directly or indirectly by the information contained in this book.

Statements made and opinions expressed in this publication are those of the author and do not necessarily reflect the views of the publisher or indicate an endorsement by the publisher.

ISBN: 978-1-957972-12-1

Illustrations by: Emily Carlin

Catnip of Life

Catnip: *an intense attraction that excites or mellows a state of mind or emotion*

Welcome to the catnip of life!
Like the effects of catnip on the cat,
reel with excitement or relax in tranquility.

Stop! Look around!
Seek something new
Listen to nature's tunes
Embrace the honeydew

Breathe three deep breaths
Release any stress
Savor the day
Take time to assess

Simple things in life
Heighten your senses
Calm your mood
Without the expenses

Observe life at its best, Listen to life's songs, Embrace life's bounties,
Breathe the breath of life, Savor life to its fullest!

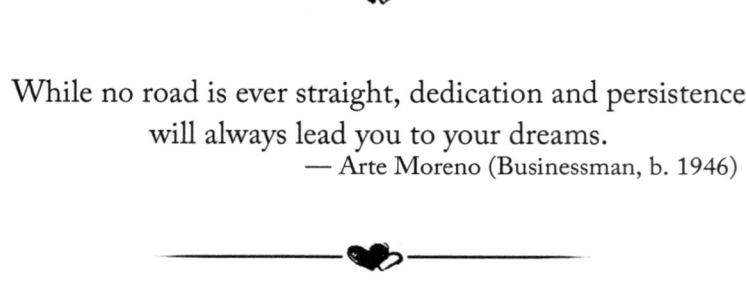

While no road is ever straight, dedication and persistence will always lead you to your dreams.
— Arte Moreno (Businessman, b. 1946)

To my daughter, Nicole Shults Reina,
who has excelled in a deaf world,
a world of little sound with abundant aspiration.

Let us be grateful to people who make us happy;
they are the charming gardeners who make our souls blossom.
— Marcel Proust (Novelist, 1871–1922)

Gratitude and Thankfulness

Through whispering angels sent from our Heavenly Father, the penning of forthcoming pages become reality. They are indeed a continuation from *His hand to mine, from my heart to yours* (*Echoes*, 2004, *Remembering*, 2009, and *Awakenings*, 2012).

Heartfelt gratefulness goes to my son, John Scott Gary, who is always supportive of his mother in her endeavors.

Dear to my heart is Andrew Lou Vickery (author, motivational speaker, retired professional baseball player), the reason catnip poetry is no longer collecting dust.

Then, genuine thanks goes to Kimberly Kirby, my techie guru, whose perseverance aligned everything when my repeated efforts were unsuccessful.

Sincere gratitude is extended to Emily Carlin, special illustrator, who's been drawing professionally for over ten years, creating art filled with youthful charm.

Thank you, my readers, for each of whom I am profoundly grateful! The written word has little meaning unless read with enjoyment and taken to heart by others.

What is life? It is the flash of a firefly in the night.
It is the breath of a buffalo in winter time.
It is the little shadow which runs across the grass and loses itself in the sunset.
— Indigenous American Saying

Contents

Introduction	17
Why Poetry	19
Why I Write	21

Observe Life at Its Best

Diamond in the Rough	25
Essence of Vision	26
Glory of the Morning	27
Cotton Candy Clouds	28
Misty Morning Fog	30
Nature's Doorway	33
Pot of Gold	34
Effervescence	36
Nature's Nightlife	38
Floratopia	40
Angels in the Snow	43
Ode to the Willow Tree	44
Catch the Falling Leaves	46
Just One Look	48
Jack Frost	50
On Top of the World	53
The Chameleon	54
Empty Nest	56
Analogy for Aging	58
Wouldn't It Be Nice	59
Witness the Wonder!	63

Mother Nature's diamonds glisten with morning dew
and sparkle in the night sky!

— *Catnip of Life*

LISTEN TO LIFE'S SONGS

Before, During, After War	67
Bells & Whistles	70
Whisperings of Nature	72
Good Ol' Days	73
Mystic Songs	74
Eskimo Kisses	77
Love, Light & Melody	78
Messages in the Wind	79
Embrace the Silence	80
Follow the Echo	82
Empty Words	85
When the Train Moves On	86
Beyond the Box	88
Outside Observer	90
Spirit of Laughter	92
Rock-a-Bye Baby	95
The Child in You	96
Healing Old Wounds	97
Forgiveness	98
Understanding	100
Heed the Voices!	104

When you wake up in the morning,
arise with thoughts of gratitude.
Open the window, listen thoughtfully with a cheerful heart!
— *Catnip of Life*

EMBRACE LIFE'S BOUNTIES

Moments Captured	109
Life's Incredible Album	110
Dew-Kissed Morning	112
Ebbs & Flows	113
Dawn 'til Dusk	114
Countless Visions	117
Somewhere Along the Highway	118
Countryside Manner	120
Life in the City	121
Eye of the Storm	122
Spirit of the Ladybug	126
Shell Island	127
Swingin' to the Rhythm of Time	128
Bona Fide Little Joys	129
C'est la vie	130
Sharing the Bounty	134
With All Things Said	135
True Riches	136
Windows to the Soul	138
Turning Thoughtfulness	140
Seize the Moment!	144

Nature swings to the rhythm of time,
echoing poetry in motion.
— *Catnip of Life*

BREATHE THE BREATH OF LIFE

Riding in the Wind	149
Mountain Air	150
Sea, Shells & Smells	152
Fantasea	154
A Walk Along the Beach	156
Smell the Rain	160
Around the Campfire	162
Festive Fête	163
Ghosts, Spirits & Cinnamon	164
Holiday Aromatic Classics	166
Somethin's Cookin'	170
Rocking Chair Motion	172
Life Smells Better without Television	174
Mother Nature's Buffets	176
Delicate Alba Rose	177
One Breath at a Time	180
Angel's Sigh	182
All in a Single Breath	184
Our Last Breath (Together)	185
Take a Deep Breath!	186
Sense the Spirit!	190

> Life is fragile. Treasure it! Nature is bountiful.
> Notice it! Awareness leads to action.
> See it . . . hear it . . . feel it!
> — *Catnip of Life*

SAVOR LIFE TO ITS FULLEST

Time Enough	195
Life's Finer Moments	196
Bears, Bees & Stings	198
At Your Fingertips	200
Savoring the Rain	202
Mystical & Magical	205
Nature's Calendar	206
Open Sky	208
Evanescent Twilight	210
Edge of Creation	212
Sometimes Life Is Lonely	215
Love's Presence	216
For the Love of You	218
If Only . . .	220
Remembering . . .	222
Thread of Life	225
Voyages: Life's Journeys	226
Aging Gracefully	228
Life Begins, Life Ends	230
Highways & Byways	232
Enjoy the Thrill!	236

Understanding nature allows you to find an empty shell and envision the life it once held while holding onto the quietude of the moment.
— *Catnip of Life*

Epilogue	239
The End . . . YOUR beginning!	241
About the Author	243

————————  ————————

Nature's peace will flow into you as sunshine flows into trees.
The winds will blow their own freshness into you,
and the storms their energy, while cares
will drop off like autumn leaves.
— John Muir (Naturalist, Author, 1838–1914)

———————— ❤ ————————

INTRODUCTION

Messages in Nature

Step outside and look around
See beyond, absorb the sound
Timeless images ne'er bid adieu
For all have messages meant for you

What do you see? What do you hear?
Visions are present loud and clear
Openness of heart amid wonder
Right before your eyes, over-under

Nature's messages—
Inspirational. Motivational.
Musical. Often whimsical.

Food for Thought:

What message does a flower send when found growing in the crack of a concrete sidewalk?

In nature, nothing is perfect and everything is perfect.
Trees can be contorted, bent in weird ways,
and they're still beautiful.
— Alice Walker (Novelist, Poet, b. 1944)

Why Poetry

Poetry is rhythmic
A melody like song
Striking the heartstrings
As life moves along

Tones are soothing
Loving sometimes
Words are healing
Calming the mind

Verses of vision
Paint a picture
Share a moment
Incite a venture

Lyrics that sing
Summon caressing
Pulse with rhythm
Become a blessing

With nature's embrace
Spirits unfold
Laughter amid tears
Capture the soul

Poetry is art. The canvas is the mind.
Thoughts are the paintbrush.
— *Catnip of Life*

The tree which moves some to tears of joy is in the eyes of
others only a green thing that stands in the way.
Some see nature all ridicule and deformity . . .
and some scarce see nature at all.
But to the eyes of the man of imagination,
nature is imagination itself.
— William Blake (Poet, Artist, 1757–1837)

Why I Write

Catnip of Life is my latest venture from a former mathematics teacher to a writer of poetry. How did it begin? Poetic math challenges, sticky notes in my children's lunch boxes, and rhythmic sayings to family and friends awakened the spirit. Then, angel whispers strengthened my ambition to complete a book of poetry, *Echoes*, 2004. In 2017, love, life, and loss intervened, changing the course of my writing altogether.

The verses of *Catnip* stir emotions resembling the effects of catnip on the cat—excite, bite, and delight—except with vision. Each poem begins with an intro and title that spark visions. These set the stage, creating a thirst for reading more and more. Within each chapter, reflection questions guide you to think about what has always been present, but maybe gone unnoticed. This is your time of personal discovery.

Poetry is perception. *Catnip's* voices speak of nature within vivid imagery. The verses give picturesque views and a way of noticing things differently. I hope to open your heart, mind, and soul to the wonder and simplicity of nature through poetry. Much remains hidden or you miss observing what is right at your fingertips, within a listening ear waiting to be welcomed.

The catnip of life bids you step away from the busyness and business of daily strife. Inspiration for poetic verse blossoms through daily walks with Mother Nature. A world where artistry is bountiful and unique, designed to be embraced.

As you read each poem, experience the journey, travel the distance line by line, where the ending is your beginning. May the words in this volume of poetry lure you to step outside and look around with gratitude for the marvels of Mother Nature.

―――――― ――――――

What is found there, in the realm of poetry,
is what is so often passed over in daily life:
the miraculous, the unexpected, the undreamt of.
— Roger Housden (Author, Speaker, b. 1945)

―――――― ――――――

OBSERVE LIFE AT ITS BEST

Life after all
Puts you to the test
What better way to live—
Observe life at its best!

Lesson from Catnip

Witness everything around you—
Up close and personal!

DIAMOND IN THE ROUGH

Quicken your steps toward thoughts of nature around you. Mother Nature is fascinating! Open your heart, mind, and soul to the natural world. Become absorbed in raw, rare, and powerful diamonds in the rough.

Raw power of nature—
Journeys of pure imagery
Mind's eye as transport
Unveils natural symmetry

Rare findings in nature—
Wonder amid fascination
Inner voices, ancient spirit
Capture sheer imagination

Powerful acts of nature—
Magic within self-awareness
Voices of nature's miracles
Heal, transform consciousness

Nature untouched, unpolished
Like a diamond in the rough
Offers better understanding—*of yourself*
Interestingly enough

Proclaim the exhilaration
Freedom deep within your soul
It's *observing life at its best*
Totally under mind's control

ESSENCE OF VISION

Mother Nature's wonder thrives where you least expect it. Uniqueness hides in yard clutter, scrubby shrubs, rocky river banks, even mud puddles. Visions of nature's spirit begin peaceful, then become powerful.

See tranquility in an overcast day
Shadowing a bench amid overgrown grass
Envision a field of purple wildflowers
Inviting wild horses to rapidly pass

Perceive rapid-flowing rivers
Cascading through rocky terrain
Imagine deafening sounds
Waterfalls, hammering rain

Stand atop a grassy hill or mountain
Scan the horizon's panoramic view
Absorb colorful magnificence
Spellbinding in watercolor hue

Observe intensely powerful currents
Beneath the vastness of ocean surf
Discover spectacular creatures
Nestled deeply within watery turf

Escape to forest wonderlands
Where creatures of nature reside
Amplify essence of vision
Let Mother Nature be your guide

GLORY OF THE MORNING

A thin, yellow curve peeps above the horizon as you stretch and yawn. Within the early hours of dawn, a symphony in outdoor surround sound bids you good morning. Birds welcome the sunrise with joyous songs . . . tune of a new day!

Morning! Dawn of a new day!
Wonder what surprise is in store
You have a prepared schedule
Enough is there no need for more

Of all important matters written down
At the top of your list let smiles abound

Day will pass by so quickly
Like the Morning Glory in bloom
Lasting for a single morning
Dying in the afternoon

Absorb the sunrise beginning each new day
Carry glory in your heart as your mainstay

Real morning splendor
Regardless of the season
Lies undaunted, breathless
Amid pied shades of crimson

Every morning greet sunrise refreshed, anew
Survey the horizon with a joyous review

Cotton Candy Clouds

When clouds are spotted, human instinct searches for familiar shapes or faces. Mere glances at clouds trigger mental images as the shapes present challenges. Instead of looking like things, many appear with angel wings.

Sunbeams emerge radiant
Upon a backdrop of blue
Then a cotton candy cloud
Adds cosmic depth to the view

In pillows of softness
Resembling feathery down
Extend quick mental images
Behind a smile, spellbound

It's a face. It's an animal.
Wild guesses engulf the scene
Evoking spirited laughter
With arguments in between

Grayness within the clouds
Changes the view altogether
Moods shift to dreariness
In approaching stormy weather

What once was cottony white
Becomes darkened and gray
Yet images still remain
Without dampening the day

Thoughts idly drift away
Fading within the hue
As cotton candy clouds
Openly fill with dew

Tears from Heaven above
Fall deftly on your face
Cleansing, nourishing
With amazing grace

Under cloudy skies
Bathed in sunshine or rain
Stirs nature's spirits
Flowing in every vein

Fluffy cotton candy clouds
Impart sheer fascination
Disclosing endless visions
Limit—*imagination*

Misty Morning Fog

Step outside on a foggy morning, and you are standing in a low cloud settled in over the Earth. Dense mist cloaks everything in sight with tiny water droplets. As ghostly apparitions appear, imagination follows. Dappled sunlight leaves you mystified.

Images appear subdued
Amidst the dense, pesky fog
Fondly kissed by stratus clouds
Disturbed by a croaking frog

Figures in the far distance
Emit varying shadowy hues
A tone so melancholy
Reminiscent of ol' country blues

Uppermost mountain peaks
Obscured by the thick fog's bed
Converge with sky's splendor
Striking gray patterns overhead

Merely a touch of fog
Steamy haze in view
Evokes mystical thoughts
Chilling through 'n' through

From the sky to the terrain
Scattering rays of sunlight drift
Semi-transparent colors emerge
As the fog doth slowly lift

In the natural world, where do you begin? Immerse yourself in words focused on Mother Nature, picturing yourself outside. As images weave through your mind, hold the visions as inspired spirits, instead of fleeting glances. Then, build upon your relationship with nature . . . how it touches your heart, how it plays a vital role. Begin sunrise with inspiration sooner than a daily occurrence fading within memory lost in time.

Inspiration

Do you witness the splendor of a sunrise or face just another day?

Splendor of Sunrise

It is morning. Just another day.
Or is it? How *do* I see it?
Rising early, sleeping late?
It's all in how I begin it.

I arise with the sun
Etching depth into the hour
Promising, eventual
Wondrous, splendid power

The sunrise—
It's gorgeous. It's glorious.
It amplifies. It deifies.

Thought for a New Day: *Keep visions forefront in your mind with the desire for further observation through a life-changing lens. See the difference!*

Nature's Doorway

Enter the natural world! Become one with nature . . . heart, mind, body, soul. Bathe in the sun's golden rays, relax to rhythmical beats, awaken your senses. Seek what happens beneath a leafy canopy, along a winding road, or during a refreshing walk.

There's a special place
You greet the rising sun
The morning air's crisp,
Lush hills ready to run

Silver mists of dew
Gleam in day's first light
Blonde honey ribbons
Reveal dawn's delight

Butterfly flutters
Tickle the nose
A place so serene
Time nearly froze

All thoughts travel
A magical distance
Dragonfly wings
Uphold faith's existence

This favorite place
Along life's highway
Mother Nature boasts
The perfect gateway

Pot of Gold

Nature tempts and tantalizes emotions. A sense of sadness arises as dark clouds drift upon skies of blue. With the sight of oncoming rain, the prospect of a rainbow brightens thoughts. The multicolor arc shifts attitudes of gray to outlooks of sunshine.

Since the beginning of time
Questions remain penned
Like how far away
Does a rainbow start then end?

The rainbow is nature's gift
After the cleansing rain
Is each one special, unique
No two ever the same?

Can the eyes of two people
Seize the same rainbow in time
Capture like water droplets
Making each vision sublime?

What makes the colors
As vivid as can be?
Are angles of light
The spectrum you see?

A red-banded outer edge
The primary rainbow posts
A reversal of color
Doth the secondary boasts

With the double rainbow
Mirror images appear
Visions of the second
Bring about quite a cheer

Seven colors of splendor
Tiny prisms beget
Orange, yellow, green
Blue, indigo, violet

A question arises
For that counts six
Have you forgotten
Red is first in the mix?

Last, above all, where oh where
Is that pot of gold?
The one you've heard about
From the days of old

It's the rainbow itself
That's the golden prize
What inspiring glory
Right before your eyes!

Effervescence

Nature's wonders appear ordinary or place you in shock. Mother Nature interjects the weird and wild into the natural world. Captivating is her charm, fiery is her anger, breathtaking is her beauty! She is the quintessence of poetry, the effervescence of life.

Transparent tiny bubbles
Those lucent little pearls
Trickle and tickle the nose
Of giggling little girls

Soap bubbles, sparkling water
Sarsaparilla, root beer
Dispense tingling sensations
Any time of the year

A twist of the wrist
Releases a soda's fizz
Hissing and spitting
All to the tune of "Gee whiz!"

Lovely bubbly champagne
Fizz everybody knows
Launches a warm feeling
Way down to the toes

Unique, lively, bubbling
Gem of a sparkling escape
Incites conversation
Leaving no room for debate

Bubbles in nature
Turbulent to serene
Dance in waterfalls
Frolic in mountain streams

Nature's bubbles
All teem with mystic glee
Bursting, popping
From highlands to the sea

Breaks in ocean waves
Iridescent seafoam
Call on each moment
That you witness alone

Colorfully prancing
Bubbles doth roll
Hear, feel, experience
Freedom within your soul

The feel of fizzy fizz
Downright incessant
Describes life at its best—
Effervescent!

Nature's Nightlife

Within soft light, dusky shadows, or stark darkness, unusual sights emerge. Nature's nightlife engulfs the scene as nocturnal flora and fauna wake up, starting their day. Enlighten your senses with a whole new perspective of the night world.

Nature by day renders amazing sights
From zesty pastels of spring
To autumn's golden delights

Butterflies amid daisies dance freehand
Dressing summer plush meadows
That stretch outward o'er the land

Wintertime glistens a personal glow
Adding magic to the air
Cool mosaics in the snow

Critters never abandoned nor alone
Robust, regal, rambunctious
Thrive in a world of their own

Ah! Such appeal by day, what of the night?
Does nature curl up and sleep
Completely out of sight?

What *is* the ambiance of life at night?
Forest, river, pond, meadow
What's in darkness to excite?

Power of the night is fascinating
Awakening somber senses
To a world captivating

Nature's nightlife renders buzzing flurry
Watching, waiting, wondering
With patience, without worry

Activity primarily at night
Hunting, scavenging, flying
Bait moments of sheer delight

Nocturnal gardens foster observing
Ugly weeds during the day
At night fully blossoming

Evening daisy chocolate flowers
Challenge the rich cocoa smells
As they play host after hours

Night owls, sleepwalkers, the insomniacs
Witness such fleeting brilliance
From dark greens to deep lilacs

Dusk 'til dawn, exotic blossoms unfurl
Quaking, twisting, popping
Within nature's night world!

FLORATOPIA

The mountain, desert, seaside, lakefront, and inland domains boast unique flora. Flowering plants, even fungi, flourish. Marine and fossil flora offer rare surprises. Each place of residency is unique. What do you know about the plant life where you live?

Splendid, copious forests
Mark regional landscapes
Impressive oaks, lofty pines
Show off stout, woody shapes

Desert plants, bright wildflowers
Pose fiery colors orange-to-red
Twisted, gnarly Pinion Pine
Claims intense green foliage instead

Deciduous trees, showy shrubs
Common to most habitats
Shed brittle leaves in autumn
Forming nature's welcome mats

Multi-faceted splendor
Fields, pastures, open ranges
Bold as though hand-painted
Once each season changes

See well beyond the obvious
Grandeur to behold
Tallgrass prairies during sunset
Glisten as spun gold

Where do you go to quiet your heart, clear your thoughts, strengthen your soul? Reading about nature, silently or aloud, opens mental gates to entryways when read with purpose—vision, insight, desire! Keep colorful images fixed in your mind and venture forth; step outside, see all that you can see. What you might perceive as trivial rocky creeks and flowing streams is the beginning of something much bigger.

Visualization

Have you thought about losing yourself in the sunset?

LOST IN THE SUNSET

Moments come to quickly go
One easily missed—a sunset
Like a retracting shadow
Or flash of a firefly when met

I watched the sun slowly descend
Became one within its glow
As its flames burst into night's calm
Absorbed its splendor and let go!

The sunset—
It's refreshing. It's replenishing.
It uplifts. It reshifts.

Thought for a New Day: *Guide your mental images toward looking for the obvious that's been in sight all along. Enjoy the excitement!*

ANGELS IN THE SNOW

A familiar winter sound is crunching of ice crystals underfoot. Laughter extends from snowflakes being caught on the tongue to throwing snowballs to creating angels in the snow. The only boundary is a blanket of white deep enough to leave an imprint.

Icy ponds form mosaics
Under the weight of sleds and skates
Hands clasp tightly, hearts melt,
Balancing two perfect soulmates

End of day sends heartbeats pounding
Racing for all our worth
Slipping, sliding, twisting
Scurrying across frozen earth

Snowflakes shine in sunbeams
Reflecting rawness of nature
Each one caught quickly disappears
Melting under pressure

A snowball fight puts us on our backs
As we giggle all the while
Eyes meet along with a gentle kiss
Ending battle with a smile

Lying on snow-covered ground
We gaze upon the sky's lustrous glow
Arms and legs reach upward, then outward
Making angels in the snow

ODE TO THE WILLOW TREE

Mother Nature announces spring with astute makeovers. Flowers in bloom, birds in song, ducks in flight appear along with windy days. After winter's last thaw, the weeping willow flaunts a flowing essence. Drooping branches become the soul of grace.

O' thou lovely willow tree
Why is it you weep?
Is it the tiny raindrops
Dancing on each leaf?

Like encircling curtains
Pendulous branches fall
Cascading slender leaves
Extend outward, droop, sprawl

O' thou drooping willow
Why do you so weep?
Are your branches heavy
From secrets you keep?

Tales, myths, sorcery
Envelop your past
Many a love spell
Romances have cast

O' you soothing sight
Why is it you weep?
Are your limbs longing
For someone to keep?

A haven of comfort
You offer each a place
Who ventures underneath
For your playful embrace

O' thou graceful beauty
Why should you so weep?
Your loveliness invites
Pleasant thoughts to keep

Cuddling within the softness
Nature provides the bed
Room to escape weariness
Close my eyes, rest my head

O' thou willow tree
I know why you weep!
Your tears are healing
So I peacefully sleep

Soft, tender caresses
Drift across my face
Offering solace
In your tender embrace

CATCH THE FALLING LEAVES

Leaf raking is rhythmic. Back-and-forth the "fingers" collect leaves before being deposited in a pile. "Get ready, get set, go!" calls for jumping right smack in the middle. Look around for your pile of leaves—what brings on smiles, giggles, hearty laughter.

If you ask me about autumn
It is leaves dancing across the ground—
Elements of a former life
Wherever nature's spirit abounds

It is one last fling before winter's sleep
Flitting, flaunting vivid hues of gold—
Dramatic, enchanting, breathtaking
Awe-inspiring persuasions to behold

It is a season of predestined change
Distinctively nature acknowledges—
Random yellows, rusty oranges, daring reds
Exciting the soul through emblazoned images

It is a time of comfort, coolness, contemplation
Leaving behind the scorching summer heat—
Switching from ice-cold lemonade to hot cocoa
Heading to the mountains for a welcomed retreat

It is daylight lessening with time falling back
Sun rising earlier, shorter days ahead—
Turning the hands of time from daylight savings
Resetting the clock before retiring to bed

It is picturesque and florid
Perfectly breathless in its prime—
Vibrantly eye-bustlingly gorgeous
Warm yet chilly at the same time

It is nature in action
Intensely, magically changing—
Summer's palette transforming
As leaves spryly fall or left dangling

It is foliage aging
Shriveling, soon browning—
Autumn's makeover
Colorfully blinding

It is multicolored leaves blowing in the wind
Like the wild strumming of a fiddle—
The crux of fun for a child to rake in a pile
Then jump right smack dab in the middle

Run, jump, catch the falling leaves
As they flutter round 'n' round
Stuff them in your pockets
For the child in you is found

Just One Look

Visions of change, glorious sunrises, and gorgeous sunsets define each season. Flora burst into bloom or go dormant as the foliage turns green or fades. Insects hatch or huddle up in hibernation. Watch for changes in birds' plumage or migration.

Just one look toward the far horizon
Absorbs an expanse beyond words
Limitless possibilities exist
Intermingled with joyous birds

Small hatchlings in the springtime
Emerge in bursts of activity
Woodpeckers' rhythmic pecking
Add drumming to the festivity

Glory in early spring
Initiates visions non-stopping
Greening hills, warming sun
Buds erupting, wildflowers popping

Family-time summer excursions
End with strolls along sandy beaches
Rising, falling blue-green sea foam
Intermittently unveils sea conches

A winding road in autumn
Demands a stop along the way
Gazing toward the earth's edge
Reveals a breathless close of day

Eye-popping scenic landscapes
Hold you utterly spellbound
Awareness demands silence
With your heartbeat the only sound

Snowcapped mountains of winter
Stand majestic out of reach
Valleys through which rivers run
Grant instant passages of each

Icy glittered scenery
Mirror iconic prisms
Shimmering in the light
Within creative schisms

Edge of sky and water connect
With discriminate attitudes
Ever present, ever-changing
Dependent upon nature's moods

Just one look first upward, then outward
Spans views altogether incredible
Senses emotionally enhanced
Emerge surprised, totally audible!

Jack Frost

The coldest season of the year brings visits from Ol' Man Winter and his pal, Jack Frost. Br-r-r cold amid snow-covered landscapes makes it tough to see past the bleakness of winter. A little imagination turns bleak colors into something of loveliness.

On a nippy wintry day
'Mid grumblesome weather
A wonderland emerges
Changing scenes altogether

Frost-laden saplings
Silhouette a blue sky
Framing frozen landscapes
Where dormant fields lie

Frozen glass wind chimes
Resemble icicles
Spiking from porch eaves
Like nature's popsicles

Magical mornings
Twinkle with silver dew
As nature's paintbrush
Wisps silently through

A pure sugary glaze
Evokes thoughts of Jack
Hugging all within sight
With his frosty attack

What enchanting visions, audible and silent, surround you? Consider morning, afternoon, twilight, and nighttime hours. Emblazoned images could be the last—seen, heard, felt, smelled, even tasted. At dawn's breaking and with lack of sunlight at dusk, there is a splendor to behold. In midday's sweltering heat or bitter cold, or during the blackest of night, wonders exist. Mysticism awaits foggy days and gray skies of stormy weather.

Enchantment

*What do fading light, dusky shadows,
or total darkness reveal for you?*

SERENITY OF NIGHT

Calmness to the night
Resides in the dusky shadows
I feel the stillness. Sense the serenity.
Quiet voices of the darkness compose

As nighttime twinkles and shines
I fall prey to the stars and moonlight
Stealthy, secretive signals
Mystify me beyond the daylight

The nighttime—
It's mysterious. It's curious.
It's amusive. It's elusive.

Thought for a New Day: *Seek something new to observe or become better acquainted with something familiar. Announce it audibly with a smile!*

ON TOP OF THE WORLD

This metaphor, on top of the world, implies the height of success or happiness. Is it your highest grade, best job position, top of the game? Consider nature: a mountain climb, rare find, excursion, or awe-inspiring view. The end mirrors your efforts; make them worthwhile.

Beyond the asphalt roads
Mule tracks provide trails
Where time seems to stand still
Wilderness prevails

Nature's glitter shimmers
Inside spacious scenes
Hiding magical wonder
In places lost between

Magical skies of awe
Reflect drama with each breath
Enticing emblazoned sights
In breadth as well as depth

On top of the world
A metaphor in disguise
Is it life's passion?
Or a view filled with surprise?

Explore new heights
Through power of the mind
Pause for the moment
Make efforts worth the climb

THE CHAMELEON

One of the coolest, most colorful reptiles on Earth is the chameleon. Quite distinctive. Most species change their skin color to be camouflaged. Making changes to fit what is "cool"—looks, likes, ideas, self—you, too, become the chameleon.

Whatever happens to be cool
May change quick as a nod
Whether in style or attitude
It's part of life's façade

Blending in with the crowd
Rallies around a time, a place
The desire to belong
Airs rather a different face

An eye in a single direction
Visions a solitary road
When the other opts not to follow
Life may well alternate its mode

An uncanny ability
Mirrors behaviors of free will
Stage acting per la naturale
Becomes a distinguishing skill

Who am I, oh, who am I?
What personas do I fancy to be?
Changes to fit a moment
Ne'er seek a permanent identity

Loner, facilitator
Wherever in life you might be
Thoughts, feelings, vibes, emotions
Remain symbolic of your ME!

Life as the chameleon
Ever changing, rearranging
Is soul connection to others
With love and new beginning

The art of concealed imagery
Lies in a familiar surrounding
A chameleon in the shadows
May be your life's new founding

Empty Nest

Kids leave home. Silence replaces echoes of pitter-pattering little feet, radios blaring, cellphones ringing, voices shouting. The empty-nest syndrome sets in. Nature reveals the sign of an empty nest when a fledgling embarking on its first flight crosses your path.

Occasionally in the outdoors
One discovers a bird's nest
Fascinating in its craftsmanship
Where speckled eggs warmly rest

Collected mud, sticks, dried-up grass
All readied for the begotten
Woven against a soft lining
Of fur, feathers, hair, and cotton

Intricacy of design
Built by two feet and a beak
Becomes nature's protector
For those which predators seek

Cradling of some smaller nests
Rests in the crook of a branch
Simple, so awe-inspiring
Like dawn at a Western ranch

Time arrives to greet the world
Peck, peck, pecking with their beaks
Air sacs pop, shells soon break
Mother Nature bespeaks

Tiny little nestlings
Eager to fly on their own
Chirping, chirping, chirping
Letting their presence be known

Baby birds flop out of the nest
Landing abruptly on the ground
Mother bird stands close by watching
In case danger might be around

After two hours of fluttering
Little birdies become airborne
Freely soaring 'neath skies of blue
A feat naturally inborn

Flying alongside their young
Parents see they get it right
Returning to their nest to rest
They sleep together through the night

Once grown flying on their own
Mother knows she did her best
Does she now somberly mourn
Facing life with an empty nest?

ANALOGY FOR AGING

Wrinkles and graying hair mark experience. Focus your thoughts away from these signs. Capture autumn leaves that drift outside your window and stroll among the wildflowers. The aging process should rest in cherished moments, rather than years.

The view atop a mountain's peak
Is void of a single word
Music of a baby's first cry—
Sweetest solo ever heard

Ocean waves during a storm
Crest majestically on their own
Vision of a child's first steps—
Rockin' 'n' reelin', never alone

Breathless skies of dusk 'til dawn
Shed brilliant hues with each view
Youth's outlook on daily life—
Promising, demanding debut

Falling leaves of autumn
Whirl whimsically through the air
Age of midlife crisis—
Unsettled over graying hair

Times for sweet reflection
Set inner smiles aglow
Twilight years of old age—
Wisdom youth should know

WOULDN'T IT BE NICE

The dictionary's biggest word contains two letters—i and f. Big, because of its implications. Perhaps you use the word without giving it much thought. What if this? What if that? Change your what-ifs to "wouldn't it be nice?" Experience the difference.

Wouldn't it be nice

. . . to catch a falling star
You could store it in a jar
To use it as a bedside light
While praying alone at night

. . . to save a lone sunbeam
It would smile a rosy gleam
Brightening each and every day
During times someone's away

. . . for the rain to never stop
You could worship every drop
Washing away inmost fears
As you bathe in heaven's tears

. . . to capture the songbird's song
You would sing it all day long
Lifting the weight within your heart
'Til better times strike restart

. . . as you foresee tomorrow
To forget the regrets and sorrow
For all the things you now have saved
Shed daily light on the path you paved

Are your visions of the world around you changing . . . more vibrant, inviting, exciting? Mother Nature has a way of whetting your appetite to discover and learn more. She arouses enhanced realization of our planet Earth, along with her vital role. Perception changes as written words summon images so striking you visualize, perceive, even smell, also taste the backgrounds. This opens the door to a desire for real-life observation.

Perception

Are trees of barren branches stripped naked of their worthiness?

THE BARREN TREE

Barren is the tree, what do I see?
Naked branches standing before me
Rough and slender stretching to the sky
Voiceless, unaware I am nearby

Scrawny little limbs are all that I saw
Mindful thoughts brought moments of awe
Where nakedness I saw, now is its plight
Poised, statuesque both day and night

The barren tree—
It strives. It survives.
It thrives. It beautifies.

Thought for a New Day: *Live your life as the tree—deeply rooted in natural charm, remaining stalwart in everything you say and do. Be diligent!*

~ Wonder of It All! ~

Dewdrops cling to a rose while a garden spider spins a silky web. A hermit crab emerges from its shell and crawls across the sand. Flora and fauna, creatures of every kind, bring you to your knees as they woo, amaze, ablaze before your eyes.

Within Mother Nature's kingdom is an incredible power of contentment. Find the light within the darkness, sweet among the sour, calmness in the furiousness, no matter the creation.

Nature is calling for you to reach out and touch it, hear it, feel it: Behold! You can almost taste it.

WITNESS THE WONDER!

Rely on your keen sense of sight—what you notice, how you perceive. Bring conscious thoughts of nature to mind daily. Witness the wonder remembering to share an experience. When you do, you communicate insight that provides awareness of life for others.

Gaze about miraculously
At nature's gifts
How mysteriously they heal
Settling life's rifts

Marvel at the moments
Mother Nature provides
Attractions richly rare
Changing with nature's tides

Treasure the scenery
In each day's delight
Relish in the splendor
From morning 'til night

Keep trusting in the morrow
Letting nothing stand in your way
Find happiness in sorrow
Behold the visions of today!

Experience Life! *Go forth. Witness the wonder!*

Go out, go out I beg of you and taste the beauty of the wild.
Behold the miracle of the earth with all the wonder of a child.
— Edna Jaques (Lecturer, Poet, 1891–1978)

Life is a song—sing it. Life is a game—play it. Life is a challenge—meet it. Life is a dream—realize it. Life is a sacrifice—offer it. Life is love—enjoy it.
— Sai Baba (Spiritual Master, 1838–1918)

LISTEN TO LIFE'S SONGS

Melodies all around
Exclaim where life belongs
Open wide your heart—
Listen to life's songs!

Lesson from Catnip

Awaken in the early hours of dawn—
Alert and powerful!

BEFORE, DURING, AFTER WAR
(Good Ol' Southern Fried Chicken)

In memoirs, before, during, and after war, amity reigned until hostility came. Then, a period of reform took place. The aftermath led folk to meet together again. Families gathered in peace as a common delight once more brought contentment—at the dinner table.

Memories echo times with friends
Teeming with smiles, joined by laughter
Families rallied together—
Morning, afternoon, thereafter

No bolts, chains held tight the doors
Open windows let in fresh air
A walk down the road came daily—
No worries, nary a care

Mom toiled alongside Pop
Resting solely when need be
Bounty of the fields flourished—
Fruits, veggies aplenty

Vital decisions before war
Found their place in the kitchen
No one argued over "first" choice—
Good ol' Southern fried chicken

Amity reigned from shore to shore
Happy were the days before war

Memories echo times with friends
Becoming few, far between
Money depleted lessened wants—
Entertainment seldom seen

News seethed of impending war
Voicing new restrictions
Daily freedoms met with restraints—
Curfews carried sanctions

Night-time raids, daily bombing, intense fear
Wreaked havoc, death in destruction
Blaring sirens were only a prelude—
A real nightmare's introduction

Meat rationed during war
Randomly found the kitchen
Everyone missed "first" choice—
Good ol' Southern fried chicken

Hostility reigned from shore to shore
Relentless were the days during war

Memories echo times with friends
Once again brimming with laughter
Families rally together—
Today, tomorrow, thereafter

Devastation in the surroundings
Overpowered a once scenic view
Time finally came for rebuilding—
Beginning again, starting anew

Rebuilding brought uniting
As people joined hands
Friends, strangers stood together—
No more battle stands

Life welcomed the normalcy
With meat back in the kitchen
Everyone agreed, "first" choice—
Good ol' Southern fried chicken

Reform reigned from shore to shore
Such were the days after war

Memories echo times with friends
Shrill as a bell's chime
Peace surely reigns within its toll
Until the next time . . .

Bells & Whistles

The steam locomotive symbolized poetry in motion. Swirls, whirls, bursts of ashen smoke invited bystanders into billowy depths. Its massive hulk eased forward with resolve, like a cat stalking its prey. Weaving along rugged terrain, it harmonized with nature's raw concepts.

Nostalgia surrounds railroad history
Poetry in motion the train displays
Steam locomotives massive hulks
Rule the rails during bygone days

"All aboard!" echoes the conductor's call
Announcing time for departure is near
Dual singing squeaks whistle through the air
Warning of motion by the engineer

A gentle tug on the throttle
The train moves forward to the call "all clear"
Stackers exhale white with black smoke
As eyes gaze upon the open frontier

Flanged wheels from front cab to caboose
Reverberate grinding metal against metal
Air brakes progressively release
Emitting shrilling, piercing noises that nettle

A black ribbon of smoke twirls, whirls, unfurls
Keeping rhythm like the beat of a drum
Cinders clatter bouncing off the cab's roof
The train roars while the rails begin to hum

Rolling down the track through darkness
Soaring across the sunny plains
The unnerving bells and whistles
Ring out even through thrashing rains

Transcontinental trains and railroads
Generate the East-West connection
Crossing mountains, digging tunnels, laying tracks
Rallying at a point of intersection

Echoes of yesteryear—May the memories prevail!

Steam locomotives no longer reign
Gone are rough rails and wooden cars
Steam no longer rises and falls
Except in historical memoirs

Lonesome bells and whistles of today
Echo sounds, evoke sights of yesteryear
Symbols of dynamic vibe, vigor
Spirited, arduous, never austere

A child thrills at such sounds within sights
. . . dreams of a keen eye upon the rail
. . . envisions a hand on the throttle
While listening to tale after tale!

Such are the memories today—May the magic recast its spell!

Whisperings of Nature

As sunbeams of energy herald day, enchanting sounds call upon the human spirit. With the drum of the woodpecker and the bumblebee's buzz, morning arrives. Inspired, you tune out mental noise and turn on whisperings of Mother Nature.

In a solemn moment
Listen for all that can be heard
'Tis outside nature calls
Without saying a single word

Recurrent rhythmic movements
Interrupt ghostly silence
Gentle winds, flowing streams
Create a peaceful ambiance

Restraint free, no limitations
Birds mimic other birds' songs
Singing upon nature's stage
Where background music belongs

Bold echoes of the sea
Recapture their home turf
Powerful yet soothing—
Whistling gusts, pounding surf

Graceful dances of the willows
Artful movements in sound
It's *listening to life's songs*—
Whisperings of nature abound!

Good Ol' Days

Among your childhood memories, perhaps you enjoyed time outdoors. Chores earned playtime in the yard, so critters 'n' things had to wait! You may declare those times bygone, but they were good ol' days. Such feelings of nostalgia personify life's songs.

As days dwindle, thoughts quickly shift
Back to the days of lesser rift

In the mind's eye, visions are clear
Of times with friends, those far, those near

The crack of dawn had us on our feet,
Completin' our chores, wantin' a treat

Off to school to wait its end
Run, run, run! Yea, home again!

Time out of doors meant climbin' trees,
Cowboys 'n' Injuns, bloody, skinned knees

Within twilight's first shadows we dawdled goin' far
Stayin' right near home catchin' lightning bugs in a jar

Rainy days, stormy days let the kitchen rock 'n' roll,
Lickin' Mom's mixer beaters, fightin' over the bowl

In the summertime nothin' beat cold chocolate milk
Suckin' on ice chips, ticklin' each other with cornsilk

Mystic Songs

Melody in nature flows freely, connecting with all life. Harmony in Mother Nature's world, even with discord, furnishes the backdrop for relaxing to intense symphonies. Birds, bees, and wind in the trees sing mystic songs day and night.

Songs of your mighty ancestors
Date back to ancient times
With melodies of lyres and harps
Long before bells and chimes

Personas of raw nature
Wonders of light and motion
Infuse form with melody
In songs filled with emotion

Caring cries of innocence
Rapt in spiritual sensations
Reveal songs of the angels
Protectful of any temptations

Songs amidst dreams
Echo of blissful flight
Veiled in shadows
Under wings of twilight

Within secrets of the earth
Inspiring tunes belong
Un-struck chords waiting beneath
Define translucence of song

Do you listen to the words as you read? Words reflect sound from your heart the same as visions in your mind. No one has the same reading experience except for frequency in reading. Reading to yourself relies on an inner voice to clarify purpose, prompt emotion. The voices become etched in the heart and burned into memory. When words recur, visions reappear, often along with attending sound.

Art of Listening

*What are your thoughts upon awakening
to the tune of the songbird?*

THE SONGBIRD

There is a bird, I hear its song
Ringing in my ears at early morn
Momentary melody, noise longtime
So I thought 'til understanding its chime

I heard the bird, understood its song
Predators it escaped all night long
Great energy it took to sing at dawn
A potential mate the sun did spawn

The songbird . . .
It pings. It sings.
It's wise. It glorifies.

Thought for a New Day: *Awaken powerfully as the songbird in the early hours of dawn. Listen attentively!*

ESKIMO KISSES

Children enjoy tickling sensations nose-to-nose that warm the heart. Such touches go beyond humans. There is the velvety nose rub with a kitten. Plus, odd couples in nature: a horse rubbing noses with a goat, a baby fox with a doe, a dog nuzzling a rabbit.

Gentle little kisses
A brush of the nose
Soft, tender caresses
Everybody knows

Language without words
Bids hello or adieu
Sweet, childlike kisses
Emanate "I love you"

Both giver, receiver
Sigh with a grin
Nuzzling on a cold day
Glows from within

Sweet, tender kisses
Forever lifelong
Whisper sweet nothings
As part of life's song

From the tiniest baby
To your most beloved pet
Little Eskimo kisses
You don't easily forget

Love, Light & Melody

Life's ups, downs, ins versus outs resemble ebbs and flows of ocean tides. Moods are light, though passionate, as melodies harmonize with crashing waves. When tempers flare, passions are in darkness, as the receding tide orchestrates with the moonrise.

Love thrives in the light
Absent of dissonant chords
Ringing poetically
Of harmonious accord

Love, light, and melody
Reside side by side
Always with ins and outs
Like the ocean's tide

Love can hurt, be blind
Leaving emptiness inside
Songs echo loneliness—
A time in life like low tide

The mirror of deepest love
Reflects emotions inside
Moments await rejoicing—
A part of life like high tide

Melodies in daily blessings
Lie voiceless inside
From grief to joy—
A fact of life like the changing tide

MESSAGES IN THE WIND

A strong breeze slaps your face, then tosses your hair in every direction possible. What is your first reaction? You dash for cover, don't you? Well, upon your next meeting, accept the gust with glee—what does the wind whisper to you?

Gentle whispers of the wind
Echo of days gone by
Unveiling nostalgic thoughts
Within a windswept sigh

Strands of tousled hair
Crisscross about the face
Swirling, twirling wisps
Completely out of place

Suddenly a burst of wind
Forces a swift brush of the hand
Providing sight of a seagull
Standing proudly in the sand

First there's only one in view
Then out of the blue there's more
Massing along the shoreline
As done many times before

Assembling in loose flocks
Each as a companion or close friend
Side by side they firmly stand
Decoding messages in the wind

EMBRACE THE SILENCE

Living commands frequent breaks with lone bits of sound. Without quiet time in your life, pleasant sounds become troubling. While taking notice of your surroundings, silence filters out the unimportant. The essential matters remain as quietude settles the mind while you listen.

Stop the restless mind
Pause mental noise of thought
Clear out the cobwebs
Day's events hath wrought

Open a door or window
Turn an ear toward the sky
Pause, listen attentively
Stare a bird right in the eye

Sit in rare silence
Hold a loved one's hand
Smile at each other
Simply understand

Speak softly as a whisper
Sing a silent song of heart
Think absolutely nothing
Tell mental noise to depart

Notice a cat's purr
Absorb the vibration
Close your eyes and smile
Adore the sensation

Go for a brisk walk
Leave the phone at home
Be watchful, patient
Enjoy time alone

Step quietly, calmly
Absorbed in rapture
Stand in the pouring rain
Smile with faint pleasure

Pick a few flowers
Stretch out upon lush green grass
Stare up at the clouds
Embrace the silence, first-class!

Silence is virtue
Unearth that which is within
With mental noise departed
Time to live again

FOLLOW THE ECHO

Murmurs of former days resound joy and sorrow, as well as joy amid sorrow. Throughout life, echoes exist as expressions of love. Profound is the mountain echo when you send and receive messages. It is soul-soothing as it connects to nature poetically.

Is it true a mountain echo
Resonates the cry of man
Swallowing up the lonely sound
Just to bring it back again?

Reflective in its harmony
Does the echo solemnly rest
On the ears of the crier
Who put it first to its test?

Somewhere in the mirrored backdrop
Of this shrill, lonely sound
Incredible beauty exists
Sometimes lost, sometimes found

Colorful rainbows, bright stars
Embroider a magnificent sky
Revealing the fragileness of life
Like wings of a butterfly

Visit the awe-inspiring mountain
Remember to follow the echo
You have but one life: *Live it!*
Applaud life's blaze all aglow

In the fussiness of everyday life, do you crave silent moments? Do chatter and clamor often overwhelm you so you need to stop and declutter your mind? Gentle voices you miss each day exist as close as a listening ear, but life's recurring events have overshadowed them. Each voice provides audible, as well as inaudible, tones. Mother Nature's world unfolds voices, gleaming with inner light, exposing sound within silence.

Moments of Quietude

Have you at times felt tossed about like riding the waves at sea?

THE CALMING SEA

Walk the seashore, hear each wave
Observe. Listen. Pause and pray.
Pounding, crashing of free will
Energy is never still

Absorb the sound. Feel its strength.
Fierce emotion in each wavelength
Crests and troughs do both reside
Ebbing with the receding tide

The sea—
It thrills. It stills.
It roars. It soars.

Thought for a New Day: *Life with its ups, downs, ins versus outs resembles the daily ebbs and flows of the ocean tides. Remain watchful of the changes!*

Empty Words

Spoken words often have no relevance other than taking up air space. Empty messages leave negative impacts, losing intentions. Weigh what you say, for when expressed, it is done. Heartfelt assurances are better than words of emptiness.

Words said with meaning
Soothe the soul, lighten the heart
Words that are mere "words"
Have no meaning from the start

Words that make no sense
Fleetingly dodge the mind
Fall on a deaf ear
No lodging do they find

Empty words are nil
Why waste the time?
Value each moment
With words sublime

Mindfulness and peace
Surround fulfilling words
Much like soulful music
Of joyous little birds

No more empty words
Should you impart
Just words with meaning
Right from your heart

When the Train Moves On

A train sits idling at a railroad crossing. The stop is irritating. You shift your weight side to side in annoyance and begin to grumble. The longer you wait, the more agitated you become. Do you consider the delay "wasted" time?

You are stopped by an idled train
What first thought comes to mind?
Unwanted, intrusive, or serene?

Hurry, hurry, hurry, move on
Words repetitive as a woodpecker
Monopolize this thought-provoking scene

Roll the window down, inhale deeply
Exhale slowly stretching arms wide
Tilt your head backward with a smile

Escape thoughtfully into nature
Ponder surrounding sights and sounds—
Artistic, expressive in style

Glance briefly in the rear-view mirror
Witness blaze of the setting sun—
Glowing, orange-red rubber ball

Shift your eyes toward the horizon
Watch rays of sunlight stretch outward—
Brilliancy, a view to enthrall

Listen to noises echo close by
Capture birds' deep guttural grunts—
Eerie, persuasive existence

Delight in surprising, mix'd tones
Greet openly music's freedom—
Intensity, pure innocence

The signal horn blows announcingly
The train slowly eases forward
Senses return to the road ahead

Final thoughts cross the empty tracks
When clearly the train has moved on—
Soul inspiration frames this railbed!

Roll the window up, exhale slowly
Inhale deeply with a final glance
As you mentally say goodbye

Mother Nature awaits your return
With amazement for tomorrow
Ease forward with a soulful sigh

Beyond the Box

Stepping outside the box moves you into unfamiliar territory. Your mindset is different, guiding your life with a new perspective. When you wake up in the morning, arise with thoughts of gratitude. Open the window, listen thoughtfully with a cheerful heart.

A room bears semblance to a box
Ceiling to floor, wall to wall
Confining that which is within
Posing little change at all

Stuck inside the box
Stifles creation
When the world outside
Erupts with sensation

Outside a bedroom window
Surfaces life beyond the box
Unfurling naturally
Without the need for alarm clocks

As daylight filters through the window
The new morning comes into view
Without scenes viewed melancholy
But as those bidding the old adieu

Greetings with the beam of light
Unite the minute your alarm rings
Little else meets early morn
Except the voice a "good morning" brings

Consider the birds as they awaken
Filling the atmosphere with song
An ambiance of joyful melodies
To carry with you all day long

Ponder how nature greets the morning
Eye the horizon, in between
What unfolds in surprising wonder
Monopolizing your first scene

Ease toward the window's light
Thwarting thoughts of the day before
Remaining stuck inside the box
This day, days to come, no more

Thoughts now align with the day ahead
Beyond the box into the light
Listening patiently, intensely
Ne'er missing a moment in flight

OUTSIDE OBSERVER

Keep a smiling face daytime and nighttime. When you sense you don't belong, become attuned to your inner self. Seek Mother Nature's signs of acceptance. With listening, hope comes with solid footprints to follow for guidance.

Are you from time to time . . .

Someone on the outside looking in
Emotionally unattached
Questioning where to begin . . .

supposedly different, apart
Awkwardly silent, all alone
Wanting to know how to start?

Do you sometimes feel . . .

Separating yourself from the crowd
Ironically with each task
Wondering what lifts the shroud . . .

whilst the feeling of being left out
Stands out like a badge of courage
Knowing how it hurts throughout?

Does life appear unforgiving . . .

When visions of hope fill with despair
Ruled by faults, fights, formalities
As misunderstandings flare . . .

while dangling at the end of your rope
Minus living, just existing
Without knowing how to cope?

Would you believe . . .

An outside observer looking in
Lives inside every one of us
Battling the daily chagrin . . .

directing change from the inside out
To bring on a smile, lift the frown
Knowing things will turn about?

Are you ready to listen . . .

To voices summoning you to hear
Glorious countryside concerts
Some faraway, many near . . .

guiding you to fields of nature-sounds
For harmonizing in the soul
Where music of life abounds?

Get ready, get set, heed Mother Nature's call!

Spirit of Laughter

Humor is the best medicine for the soul—never dreaded, nor does it require hours or overnight to take effect. It carries a no-cost price tag, no prescription. Joyous side-splitting laughter brings tears to your eyes as you fall to your knees laughing at yourself!

Spirit of laughter
From the inside out
Echoes emotion
Gladness brought about

Laughing and crying
Offer release, relief
Connecting to others
As you smile or weep

During difficult times
Pause, stop, look all around
Delight in life's treasures
Listen for happy sounds

Whether the day before
Or the morning after
Humor lifts the spirit
As smiles emit laughter

Laughter never ages
Grabs heartily at your sides
Knows no boundaries
Bridges the deepest divides

Would you agree visions within quiet voices are heartfelt? What lies within the heart remains in the heart, good or bad, happy or sad. Allow whatever enters your heart to accept love, joy, peace, rest, and solitude. Know life's songs carry many hearty messages. To soothe. To heal. Yes, even to hurt. Permit those carrying hurtful tunes to find solace among the voices of Mother Nature. Find comfort in nature's retreat.

Take It to Heart

Do you consider yourself a wandering soul?

A Soulful Heart

I wondered about the microcosms of nature
I pondered their connection to human life
Then I wandered into Mother Nature's arms
With reassuring inspiration amid strife

There I discovered my wandering soul
Being heartfully blessed beyond words
Enthused voices of flora and fauna
Melodious tunes of joyous birds

A soulful heart . . .
It's open. It's unbroken.
It's resonating. It's contemplating.

Thought for a New Day: *Venture forth heartily with all the newness you have gathered in the forefront of your mind. Let heart and soul remain connected!*

Rock-a-Bye Baby

As an infant, loving arms offered comfort. When growing up, you encountered bumps and falls. With each break in rhythm, someone stood by until one day you stood tall on your own. Now your growth repeats itself through your children and grandchildren.

Rock-a-bye baby cradled in mother's arms
Rests safely above ground away from all harm

Ambitions lifted high *on the treetop*
Become dream's reality never to stop

With stormy times, inside is peaceful, still
When the wind blows life resounds chilling, shrill

In midst of opposition or a stumbling block
Straight away or crossroads *the cradle will rock*

The foreboding words *when the bough breaks*
Bittersweet at best the path life takes

Loving and tender that's the choice for life's song
The cradle will fall is daunting all day long

From birth to grave many problems shall befall
Down will come baby—ready to withstand all!

The Child in You

Regardless of age, a child lives within. Days exist when the kid inside lies dormant, memories blur. Other times, a blanket wraps the child with comfort in memory of bruised egos and skinned knees. The core of your youth keeps what you once were alive.

When you were young
Life seemed without a care
Filled with giggles
Watchful with every dare

Subtle, vibrant, elusive
Were adventures of the day
Where the obvious, the dull
Never were parts of the play

Now that you are older
Gone, the quirky childish games
For life has new meaning
Altogether different aims

With the aging process
Gone should never be
That which keeps you alive
The child in you on key

Subtle, vibrant, elusive
Be adventures of today
Where the obvious, the dull
Remain absent from the play

HEALING OLD WOUNDS

The unexpected may cause heartache. Solitude is sought, no disruption. In quiet thought, a glance through a window discloses abundance surrounding you. When sadness comes, seek solace from nature that produces cheery thoughts to turn frowns into smiles.

When your heart's broken
Where's the end to the pain?
Life seems uncertain
Lost in eternal rain

Loneliness, your companion
Resides in clouds of gray
The question of every hour
"When will it go away?"

Time for healing
Reflects on life's test
All the heartache
Must be laid to rest

Life's song of pure joy
Simply hit a sour note
A dream still believed
Remains far not remote

Voices of bygone days
Now bring sunshine after rain
Time for healing old wounds
Restores faith in love again

FORGIVENESS

Do roses prick honeybees for stealing tiny drops of nectar? Are trees blaming the wind for bare or broken branches? Do birds forgive what disturbs their nests? In nature, there are only aftereffects. Consider the consequences if forgiveness is void in your life.

Are you willing to forgive
Void of a snappy reply?
Do you play the blame game
When something goes awry?

Forgiveness reaches out with open arms
Transcending momentary weeps
To quickly resolve misunderstandings
Instead of remaining for keeps

Gentle hugs transmit a warm message
Overcoming involuntary tears
To suddenly settle differences
Before they continue for years and years

Expressions of comfort bring peace
Conquering innermost doubts
To nimbly end bitter disputes
Without any need for shouts

The hand of friendship stretches forth
Touching the grief-stricken heart
To kindly ease the throbbing pain
With promise of a new start

Where would you be without forgiveness?
Lost and alone, stubborn and frail
Living life without sincere meaning
Waiting for the end of life's trail

Forgiveness stems from true spirit
Descending deep into the soul
To lay the path for shared consent
Never separate, always whole

Incredible power of forgiving
Letting go yet still remembering
Shows the inner beauty of forgiveness
Easing the pain, numbing the trembling

Heart and soul go hand in hand
Binding togetherness
To bring peace within hard times
No blame, just forgiveness

UNDERSTANDING

Life throws erratic curves. Reactions vary with decisions sometimes being wrong choices. Help is needed to cope with heartache or distress. Mother Nature offers comfort. Listening requires no judgment and understanding lives in your heart.

Have you done things you are ashamed of
Asked forgiveness from Heaven above?

Have you buried them deep in your heart, your mind
Keeping them harbored, wanting no one to find?

Have you coped daily seeking others to ease pain
Unknowingly hurt loved ones but wanted to blame?

You need to find a way to dry boundless tears
Unleash hidden secrets, end nightmares and fears

Healing comes slowly progressing through each day
Words are hard as emotions get in the way

To forget may be impossible
To forgive, hopeful for mankind

With understanding the main concern
Kindheartedness heals heart and mind

Walk with Mother Nature, have a conversation
Remain grateful, write your own healing quotation

No better listener who carries no judgment
Openly allowing healing with contentment

Do you recognize that voices in nature serve to love and heal? Melodic tunes emerge from many sources. Each refrain has its own voice, a singular story, a soul-clutching song. Some lie dormant, waiting to be awakened—heartfelt and soul-filled. Others announce their presence with jubilance, often brushed aside as noisiness. Such is melody. Such is life. Each has its place on the staircase leading to everlasting joy.

Unchain the Melody

What does the voice of a seashell whisper to you?

THE SEASHELL

I found a seashell, what did I hear?
Melody came when put to my ear
Its journey from sea towards land
I never took time to understand

I found a new seashell, what did I see?
Life it once held, its voice formerly
For the shell to surface with the tide
Death of a mollusk happened inside

The seashell—
It's beautiful. It's bountiful.
It's tiny or fat. Once a habitat.

Thought for a New Day: *Strengthen your approach to listening to life's songs, focus on the recurring voices. Relish every single note!*

~ Voices to Be Heard! ~

Among nature's cries and whispers, voices lie filled with soulful spirits that strike the heartstrings. They yield a symphony of tender notes or roar with thunder. Awareness deepens as the mind absorbs the sound. Yet, buried inside any noisiness, silence exists.

Nature's voices compel you to enter the kingdom of wonder. Within its splendor, the natural world marks a seasonal change with a spring or summer rain. Lightning flashes nearby, shocking thoughts back to reality.

Listen to the voices of Mother Nature.
Many bursts awaken your senses with revelation!

HEED THE VOICES!

Without television, cellphone, and tablets, focus shifts to voices of nature. Their messages guide your every movement and engage your innermost thoughts. When all things sing, you find comfort in grief while adrenaline pumps in happier times.

Melodic harmony in song
Begins with quiet repose
Ends with energies electric
As emotion grows and grows

All things possible
Exist through tuneful song
Strumming the heartstrings
Where promises belong

Sunshine in the daytime
Refreshes and relieves
Gracing nature's mats
Of flowers and leaves

Frequent in starless nighttime
Moonlight serenades exist
Melodies envelop passion
No one can willingly resist

Pitter-patter of rain
Like the beat of a drum
Pulses rhythmically
Adding to nature's hum

Such melodious songs of life
One note to another
Harmonize camaraderie
Soul sister to brother

When all things sing
Even least of the least
Hearts are at rest
Spirits soar, souls at peace

Experience Life! *Go forth. Heed the voices!*

When we pay attention to nature's music, we find that everything on the Earth contributes to its harmony.
— Hazrat Inayat Khan
(Founder and Teacher of Universal Sufism, 1882–1927)

Forests, lakes and rivers, clouds and winds, stars and flowers, stupendous glaciers, and crustal snowflakes—every form of animate or inanimate existence leaves its impress upon the soul of man.
— Orison Swett Marden (Author, 1848–1924)

Embrace Life's Bounties

Life's small treasures
Lay hidden in the remotest counties
Never let them go unnoticed—
Embrace life's bounties!

Lesson from Catnip

Realize little things make a difference—
The evanescent and eternal!

MOMENTS CAPTURED

Sunny days or somber skies invite chances to capture life in "moment" time. No sooner one sighting comes, something unexpected emerges. Split seconds may be a beginning, others an end—joyful morsels that nature brings.

Witness life in the moment
From morning dew to midnight sky
A surplus of snapshots exist
Viewable with the naked eye

Above distant silhouetted trees
Diffused rays of sunlight emerge
Beetles nibble lush foliage
As senses of nature's splendor surge

Tiny hummingbirds hover
Flying backward at lightning speed
Vivid iridescent plumage
Brilliant throat color flash indeed

Frogs break the silence
Croaking live-band entertainment
Joyous morning songbirds
Chirp a unique arrangement

Angels of light appear
Casting sunbeams early morning brings
Ladybugs feed on aphids
Capturing moments beneath their wings

LIFE'S INCREDIBLE ALBUM

Mother Nature shines with joy and cries in sorrow as sunshine is mixed with its share of rain. The sunbeams provide glowing comfort while the raindrops refresh. Beams bring happiness inside and out. When tears come, the heart is strong with nature's rhythmical beats.

Life's a trail of tears
The will to cope
Met with discomfort
Grounded in hope

It's a highway of dreams
A road demanding
Out of balance at times
Yet understanding

Time's journey
Casts shadows of despair
Wants, desires
Times totally unfair

Life's bounties
Pose gifts to share
Ready to be opened
Handled with care

A kitten's purr
A dog standing guard
Such is life's blessing
In your backyard

Mountains, forests
Meadowlands, seaside
Time's passages
Lead you far and wide

Family and friends
Cherish life's relationship
Spirits reunite
Openly in fellowship

Life's an incredible album
Of sad and joyful times
Echoing of discordant notes
And melodious chimes

Life's a trail of laughter
Zealous to smile
An ocean of comfort
Making life worthwhile

It's a highway of dreams
A road demanding
It's *embracing life's bounties*
With understanding

Dew-Kissed Morning

Ruffled rose petals emit a slightly spicy scent radiating the presence of love. Each color carries a unique message. Tears accompanying the rose revitalize the inner spirit much like the morning dew quenches the rose's thirst.

Sparkling, dancing dewdrops
Sway lazily with a slight breeze
Falling deftly to earth
Lightly touching petals and leaves

Dew's misty water droplets
Quench life's thirsty pups
Resting on a spider's web
Before sunlight erupts

Dew-laden leaves and foliage
Grace picturesque scenery
Within morning visions
Of pearlized greenery

Pale light casting soft shadows
Enhances morning hue
As nature's teardrops
Reflect day's first hints of blue

Delightful dew-kissed morning
Magical, blissful in view
Rekindles inner thoughts
As the rose opens wet of dew

Ebbs & Flows

Within life are journeys, challenges, memories—and obstacles. Each involves inspiration captured from the ebbs and flows of life. Moods change like the ocean's tide, whispering of the past within echoes of each crashing wave.

Ebbs & flows of the sea respond to the sun and moon
Whispering of the past to crashing waves' tireless tune

Hearts & souls of the sea in sepulchers of the deep
Lie fearless of pounding sounds obdurate rocks unleash

Bells & horns of the sea resonate across the waves
Resounding things forgotten to shun watery graves

Gulls & dolphins of the sea frolic beneath afternoon sun
Plunge-diving into crashing surf as baitfish stay on the run

Starfish & sea urchins of the sea with exotic spiny skin
Lie dormant at low tide awaiting collection to begin

Shells & smells of the sea resound of sweet, salty air
Voicing bold, vibrant remembrance way beyond compare

Moonbeams & winds of the sea beckon songs waves compose
Thoughts harken to the night pondering life's ebbs and flows

Highs & lows of life mimic ebbs and flows of the sea
Ups and downs, ins and outs, rhythmic changes meant to be

Dawn 'til Dusk

Have you paused with notice to the difference between morning twilight that ends with dawn and evening twilight that ends with dusk? As darkness falls, shadows of nighttime cast their characters in harmony with the moon and twinkling stars.

Whispers of Dawn . . . awaken a new day
Pre-dawn maiden colors replace night's gray

Figures of first light dance furtively into view
Bold spectral effects fade into metallic blue

Heat of Midday . . . radiates sunlight's glare
Soft effortless colors poise in midair

Cool midday breezes diminish afternoon heat
Allusions of rain render day's ending complete

Peace of Twilight . . . finds quietude in play
Serene red-orange hues stage a ballet

Surreal saffron casts an illusionary show
Soft billowy clouds reflect the sun's fading glow

Songs of the Night . . . harmonize in the soul
Melodic symphonies tease and console

Subdued radiance slowly transcends the darkness
Night comes, light goes in awe of bittersweetness

Are you wealthy? Embracing life's bounties doesn't mean hugging a money bag every morning you wake up and each evening when you retire. Loving money is good, but remember, it's all in how you view its value. Embracing life's bounties starts each day with a grateful heart. Being bountiful places you in the giving and receiving end of life's treasures—open and receptive to the abundance of the universe.

Bountiful Treasures

How often do you embrace the little things that are bountiful?

NATURE'S TREASURES

A treasure trove of wonder
That's nature's sights and sounds
Nurturing both heart and soul
With glory that abounds

Sightings of splendor
Beacons they provide
Shining day and night
Always as your guide

Nature's treasures—
Joy in her kingdom. Pearls of wisdom.
Sunrise in its glory. Mother Nature's story.

Thought for a New Day: *Remain joyous of heart, smiling in the moment, and optimistic in the glories of life. Collect nature's pearls!*

COUNTLESS VISIONS

Countless visions fill the mind representing relationships with nature's world. It's up to you to capture the splendor breaking forth within awe-inspiring views. Never being fully defined, they are ever-changing, bringing something new into view.

Across the vast expanse of wide-open seas
Lie seemingly endless canvasses of blue

Countless visions of masterful beauty
Laud His presence powerful, pure, and true

At dawn, morning glories bloom
With dew quenching nature's thirst

Countless visions of life's existence
Bare His glory stirring, set to burst

Somber shadows beneath a cloud-filled sky
Offer shelter as stormy winds draw near

Countless visions of assurance with protection
State His presence majestically, loud and clear

Imminent tranquility once the storm has passed
Reflects awe as I ponder what's in life for me?

Unknown is exactness of the time or place
Countless visions secure faith eternally

SOMEWHERE ALONG THE HIGHWAY

America, the Beautiful *is depicted in general conversation, poetic verse, essays, magazines, books, film, and song. One of America's icons is amber waves of grain: the vastness of field after field of amber-colored wheat located across America's Great Plains.*

Somewhere along the highway
Lay fields of amber durum wheat
Where ghostly footsteps long past
Tread lightly among slender stalks

Across the American plains
Sometimes amid a backdrop of hills
Spreads miles of massive acreage
Colorful as trees and daffodils

Visions unlock scattered memories
Of holidays in the countryside
Within the ardor of autumn's
Noonday siestas, midday walks

No photographs, no diaries,
Only fading memory at its finest
Connects past with the present
As you ponder to still remember

Brisk winds brush the slender spikes
Rippling grains like disturbed water
As golden wheat's autumn setting
Reflects blushing September

A sight to behold
Glory in your midst
Dancing within the breeze
Delicately sun-kissed

Somewhere along the highway
Picturesque scenes appear
Field after field sparkles
Being touched by misty rain

The tall slender stalks
Sway within the mist
Cueing the icon
"Amber waves of grain"

Countryside Manner

Pictures have a way of soulfully drawing you right into the scene. The image is so vivid, so persuasive you feel as though you are there. It could be you've imagined a setting. It becomes implanted in your mind where nothing can stop you from searching for such a place.

Vast webs appear strung
With beads of morning dew
As the sun emerges
At the bottom of the sky

An oratorio of croaking frogs
Birds, mammals, creepy-crawlies
Permeate the air with song
Initiating a fond youthful sigh

Expanses of green on green
Adorn the rolling hillside
As wildflowers, gems of beauty
Join the horizon's edge of blue

Horses graze in a circular pattern
Alongside a field of buttercups
A farmhouse stands in the background
While chickens lay eggs in plain view

Such is countryside manner
Where thoughts lost in daydreams
Leave imagination unbounded
On wings completely free

LIFE IN THE CITY

Are you country born, country stayed or city born, city to this day? Much is to be learned from both sides of life. The sleepy countryside isn't for everyone nor is hectic city life. One may seem pale in comparison to the other. Seek brightness of each.

Welcome to the city! May I show you around?

A concrete jungle it has long been called
A mighty fortress towering, stone-walled

Glaring, surely blaring, sights amid sounds
All around the city hold you spellbound

Daytime, nighttime makes you feel like new
Singing, dancing, nothing you can't do!

Hustling, bustling, crisscrossing asphalt streets
Busy coffee shops welcome all to meet

Spectacles, odd routines invite strangers to stroll
Events in a city park offer a grassy knoll

A haven for many, sin city to a few
Life in the city never bids adieu!

Hello to the city! Ready to wheel around?

Hail a taxi in a heated rush
Paint the city with your own life's brush!

Eye of the Storm

The time before a storm is quiet with contemplation. Within the storm's fury, the center reflects calmness known as the eye. Once it passes, stillness returns, and the aftermath awaits healing. So goes Mother Nature—so goes human nature!

Beneath calm skies . . .

Nature's sunbeams indescribably dance
With panoramic magnetism at a glance
Sun-kissed colors beyond imagination
Create timeless scenes of fascination

Within gray skies . . .

Imminent changes in weather conditions
Open your senses to nature's musicians
A chill creates goosebumps under the skin
Increasing intently with the blowing wind

During pouring rain . . .

Lightning strikes, thunder claps
Snapping, tearing sound perhaps
Rain beats down upon the earth
Eager for life's rebirth

In the eye of the storm . . .

True calmness exists behind closed eyes
Amidst balmy winds, clear blue skies
Fauna appear after the first welter
Only too soon to again seek shelter

After the rain . . .

Nature's teardrops adorn the scene
Settling down betwixt and between
Drip, drip, one then two
Blinks of shiny dew

At any given time . . .

Nature can be soft, gentle, benign
Waiting, wanting nothing of mankind
Like humans it can turn in an instant
Become intense, aggressive, persistent

How do you connect to Mother Nature's charm in terms of grace? Grace is anywhere you accept its subtle presence. Walk along a wooded path, rest upon a felled tree, become absorbed in nature's bounty where gracefulness is at hand, step-by-step. Listen. As your mind collects visions, store the images as memories for later recall. Inner voices keep them tuned to nature, giving mental thoughts a break from daily stress.

Gentle Grace

What is your experience with Mother Nature at moments of grace?

GRACE

The epitome of grace stands before me
Surrounding the heart of everything I see
Over the land, upon the sea, in the trees
Amid a storm or within a lulling breeze

What moments of grace gently stand before you?
The unspoiled raw quintessence of skies of blue
With morning visions of pearlized scenery
Await your attention unquestioningly

Grace—
It moves. It soothes.
It encases. It embraces.

Thought for a New Day: *Cast your thoughts upon serene waters where the slightest ripple produces a promising outcome. Embrace graceful moments!*

Spirit of the Ladybug

Have you had a ladybug, ladybird, or lady beetle rest upon your shoulder or tickle your palm? Regardless of its name, this wee bug is an insect, but one connected to the balance of life. Ladybugs mirror good fortune and positivity, and link to divine ideals.

Ladybug, ladybug, what do *you* see?
As I gaze upon you do you see me
Watchin' for fragile wings to emerge
Stirring zestful emotions that surge?

Prayerfully I wish for you to stay
Then a raindrop whisks you away
Come back, come back my little friend
Across seas of grasses tall 'n' thin

Barer of wisdom joyful in flight
Release your spirit into the light
Tickle my palm, sit tight on my knee
On my shoulder I welcome thee

Ladybug, ladybug what do *I* see
As I gaze upon you lookin' at me?
A creature so tiny, delicate too
Captivating soulfully through 'n' through

Herald of promise a great spirit to behold
All in the revelation of the ladybug's soul
The ladybug's message along any path trod
Humbly powerful to "let go and let God"

SHELL ISLAND

Offshore islands make charming habitats. When walking the shoreline, one finds sand dollars and shells that whisper of the sea. Sandpipers scurry along pecking debris as waves retreat. Voices of Mother Nature stay long after footprints wash away.

Swimmers dodge the breaking waves
As beach blankets lay scattered about
Wave runners motor offshore
Weaving vigilantly in then out

With each break of the crashing surf
Sandy crabs return to the sea
Retreating tide pulls them backward
As kids' tiny feet jump with glee

Carefree voices echo along the shore
With each attempt to jump the roaring swells
Zesty aromas permeate the air
From salty sea spray to raw ocean smells

Local beach hounds carefree as can be
Run friskily in and out of the surf
Frolicking, catching Frisbees 'n' things
With no desire to return to home turf

Walking the beach uncovers seashells
Washed ashore with the receding tide
Footprints in the sand soon disappear
With fond memories left to reside

SWINGIN' TO THE RHYTHM OF TIME

An old spare tire might swing in your memory. Its rhythm stays in sync, gliding backward, forward. Often, it shifts from side to side. Throughout life, rhythms are in harmony or become fragmented. The rhythm slows, leaving cherished memories.

The backyard is quiet
Now that we are alone
Kids are all grown up
Moved out, on their own

Days are lingering
Night much too long it seems
Laughter in the backyard
Only in our dreams

Lasting memories
Of childhood, I reminisce
Barren trees silhouette
Times ne'er gone amiss

Twilight's silver lining
Soft backdrop for the ol' elm
Renders time motionless
Poised in an enchanted realm

Wispy, melancholy thoughts
Shift back and forth within my mind
Visions of that old spare tire
Swingin' to the rhythm of time

BONA FIDE LITTLE JOYS

Bygone days left no stone unturned or ignored. Imagination reigned, outdoors ruled without techie devices. Pranks were innocent fun, and today you state many times, "I can't believe I ever did that!" Whether creator, ringleader, or witness, lasting marks remain.

What is childhood
Without feisty tales?
Eating dirt, chasing crickets
Where's Sammy the snail?

Running carefree about the house
Out of control, slamming doors
Outside from morning to night
Where are the enchanted swords?

Swinging in the backyard
Carving notches in tree bark
Packing fruits and veggies
To feed wildlife in the park

Romping with Mother Nature
Catching lizards by the tail
Watching Daddy's reaction
To the outdoor sign "for sale"

Bursting into laughter
Generating noise, noise, noise
Dirty hands, smudged faces
All bona fide little joys!

C'EST LA VIE

The French idiomatic expression c'est la vie means it is the life or that's life. Casual conversation often includes the phrase in rebuttal, agreement, sarcasm, or regret. It conveys that is just how things happen in life.

Mix-ups, squabbles, and spats
Inherent each seems
For everywhere you turn
None less the extremes

Confusion regarding naught
Pleads answers to questions
Nagging at uncertainties
Begs any suggestions

Emotions soar, tempers rise
Right on the verge of screams
Perplexed, twisted spiral
Bickering toward extremes

Quarreling over surely nothing
In itself another extreme
Conjuring up backbiting words
Begetting nightmares, rather than dreams

Extremes are of your making
Down to points of silence
Wanting to avoid a scene
Stillness thwarts violence

Where do you go for stillness?
Seek solace from deep within
Look for contentment inside
Try a new way to begin

Try, try, try with all your might
'Til calmness overcomes bane
Silent emotions take hold
For you tried, tried, tried again

Such is what you confront
In the midst of daily strife
Mix-ups, squabbles, and spats
C'est la vie—that's life!

Survey Mother Nature's realm
Find solace within her fold
Comforting is her nature
Instead of a heart stone cold

Do you recall the first time Mother Nature held you in her grasp? Did you notice a budding flower of spring or autumn's falling leaves? Perhaps you dug your bare toes in dew-dappled grass or encountered a summer grasshopper. Maybe the winter sun eased into view along dawn's horizon or descended at the close of day. Or possibly the voices outside your window echoed melodic tunes of the natural world.

Precious Moments

What is your most memorable momentary encounter with nature?

CAPTURING THE MOMENT

Rapture existed in the moment
Capturing my thoughts amusingly
As a two-striped pink grasshopper
Lazily sunned itself in the sand

Moments are swift, fleeting
Like the flight of a dragonfly
The delight in nature—
Humor underfoot and at hand

The moment—
It arises. It passes.
It invites. It excites.

Thought for a New Day: *Broaden your intuitive nature-capturing moments toward a better understanding of the world around you. Discover your inner self!*

SHARING THE BOUNTY

Mother Nature's world triggers caring moments that set an example. Nurturing the young creates thoughts of love and comfort. Embrace what is around you for kind gestures yield good vibrations. There's hidden power in kindness—from Mother Nature to human nature.

Kindness of the heart
Says a lot void of words
Like joyful spirits
Propelled by little birds

Such actions extended
Happen without thought
Coming naturally
Instead of being sought

Giving requires no looking back
That comes as no surprise
Whenever sharing the bounty
Look right before your eyes

One may appear to have a lot,
Some little to spare
It's the little that have a lot
When willing to share

Reflect upon yourself
Short- and long-range . . .
How often have you said
"Please, keep the change"?

WITH ALL THINGS SAID

Throughout life, success meets obstacles plagued by, "Will I make it this time?" followed by, "Why try?" You know why. You have overwhelming zeal, passion, to live a dream. Then, unyielding grit, tenacity, to see it happen.

Seems too many wrong things
Always appear in the scene
When more of the right things
Need a way to intervene

Life's ultimate dream—
A world without fear
Variance in direction
Falls on the listening ear

Tests of patience, endurance
Plague mankind from the start
Meeting with understanding
Settles differences of heart

The way may seem lost, heartless
Changes in course the scene
The dream awaits you there
Could be upstream or downstream

*Life is so short, often abrupt
With all things said, never give up!*

TRUE RICHES

Wherever you are, whatever you are doing, pause thoughtfully naming what makes you truly grateful. You may find the naming simple or discover it takes time, also effort. Regardless of easy or hard, the goal is gratefulness for yourself plus everything you have.

Consider that which makes you grateful
What would be at the top of your list—
Friends, family, loved ones, favorite pet
Something you simply love to persist?

Material—here today, gone tomorrow
Proposes value void setting in stone
But when it comes to everlasting life
It is priceless—it and it alone

Life is filled with amazing bounties
Each to be considered on its own
To be thought incredible
Measured from birth until grown

As a tiny infant you learn dutifully
Survival outside your mother's womb
With loving care, nourishment of adoration
You grow up going forth in full costume

From childhood to young adult
Life flows like a river of dreams—
First crush, first date, first kiss
Without worry or so it seems

Once into the world of adulthood
Life takes on a whole new meaning
Gratefulness is the bounty of life
Which is only the beginning

As the days turn into months
The months forge ahead into years
Passing by all too quickly
Memory slowly disappears

The tick-ticking hands of time
Move in only one direction
The only way to step back
Is merely in life's reflection

Live each day for its moments
Rather than day by day
True riches of life excel
In all you do and say

Windows to the Soul

Within your body dwells a spirit of heart, heart of soul. Each part functions from the heart—seeing, speaking, listening, feeling. The heart speaks; the soul listens. Windows open to one day close, with each closing setting the stage for a new opening.

Eyes twinkle as smiles unfold
Opening windows to the soul

Lips of kindness softly speak
Shedding wisdom for the meek

Ears capture thoughtful sound
Mellowing voices that surround

Sights and sounds of nature's rare beauty
Keep you attuned to faith and duty

Arms stretch outward opening wide
Inviting warmth for comfort inside

Hands keep loved ones secure when near
Clasping tightly those truly held dear

Legs and *feet* a firm foundation stand
Holding faithfully through each demand

Mind and body together remain in sync
Being in control of what you do and think

Heart with emotion triumphs to never subside

Waning not, enduring forever to abide

Spirit of devotion joins family in hand
Echoing solidity without shifting sand

Soul in tune with the heart rings deep
Affirming passions as you sleep

Mindfulness unites the heart with the soul
Awakening thoughts to never grow cold

TURNING THOUGHTFULNESS

Hot, dry spells make you thankful for the rain, while during winter, it's when falling snow wanes. The nurture Mother Nature brings provides thankfulness for the value of the natural world. Thus, you express gratitude for the blessings received.

Be thankful for many blessings
Each new day may impart
Specially those unexpected
Which arrive heart to heart

Be thankful for troubled times
Reaching out to those concerned
For with painful mistakes
Lessons can certainly be learned

Be thankful for little things
From strangers and loved ones alike
Whose genuine thoughtfulness
Presents a delightful heartstrike

Be grateful for nature each morning
With which a fresh start begins
Giving thanks for natural blessings
Until the day finally ends

Turn thoughtfulness into gratitude
A work of heart, a drill of soul
Find pleasure giving to others
A notion to never grow cold

What is the distinction between thanking someone and expressing gratitude? As a child, an awareness began for noting thankfulness. Being thankful became the first step. Your heart spoke when "Thank you" followed a kind gesture. As an adult, you express gratitude, recognition for all you have in life. Gratitude changes everything as you realize life's true riches. You learn to be thankful, while you choose to stay grateful.

Gracious Gratitude

When/where do you behold kindness in nature?

A GRATEFUL HEART

Me, my, mine
Words at chosen times
One by one
Miss important signs

Emotions of the heart
Kindled by amusive facts
Sparkle among nature
In win-win kindness acts

A grateful heart—
It's kind. It's thankful.
It's bubbling. It's humbling.

Thought for a New Day: *Embrace kindness with a grateful heart, remaining observant of the little things that make a difference. Capture the moment!*

~ Moments Captured! ~

A soft haze drifts across the lake. Through the mist, faint sunbeams cover you as a warm cloak would drape your shoulders. Tadpoles wiggle in the early light as you peer downward.

You lay aside your shoes, sit on the end of the dock, and dangle your legs over the edge. You let your toes swish backward, forward on top of the cool water. As ripples disturb the serenity, scenes of tranquility surround you. You sigh.

Capture picture-perfect images of a rare find:
Store mental pictures in the scrapbook of the mind!

Seize the Moment!

An odd sound strikes an unfamiliar chord or you glimpse something unexpected. In a flash, gone! These are fleeting moments—captured, caught, lost as swiftly as they occurred. Opportunities fade, but regret can last a lifetime.

At a moment's notice
Life tosses a surprise
With little warning
Right before your eyes

Wait a moment you say
But waiting's not to be
What's about to appear
May flit before you see

A fleeting moment
Passing without notice
Misses the realm and
Splendor of blue lotus

Present, painful, passive
Brief periods of time
Moment to moment
Meaningful and prime

An awkward moment
Could catch you off guard
Whether right or wrong
It's like a flashcard

Moments come, moments go
Like the blink of an eye
You catch them or you don't
As they swiftly fly by

Images of simple moments
Enter scrapbooks of the mind
Soundless, motionless
Waiting to rewind

Experience Life! *Go forth. Seize the moment!*

We don't remember days. We remember moments.
— Cesare Pavese (Novelist, Poet, 1908–1950)

Nothing is more memorable than a smell. One scent can be
unexpected, momentary, and fleeting,
yet conjure up a childhood summer
beside a lake in the mountains.
— Maya Angelou (Poet, 1928–2014)

BREATHE THE **B**REATH OF **L**IFE

Life's inherent nature
Commands daily strife
Relax, inhale deeply—
Breathe the breath of life!

Lesson from Catnip

Recognize Mother Nature's perfumes—
Both opulent and subtle!

RIDING IN THE WIND

Air in motion is invigorating! Winding through Mother Nature's corridors brings you closer to nature's elements. As wind blasts across your face, a sense of freedom engulfs your soul. The sting of the wind produces refreshing sensations, rather than pain.

Warm sunbeams seep into the skin
Wispy strands of hair blow in the wind
Puffy clouds upon cerulean blue
Amplify an imaginative view

Countryside, mountains, rivers, and streams
With/without Mother Nature's extremes
No matter the season, calm or stormy
Just being outside, sultry or balmy

Along the highway spans open fields
Tempting sensations to turn the wheels
A farmhouse abandoned in the distance
Emits auras of peaceful existence

Cornfields behind, dense forests ahead
Critters scamper seeking nature's bed
A doe and her fawn nibbling at leaves
Quickly disappear among the trees

Overwhelmingly life's magnificence
Personifies nature's significance
Any time beyond vacation or weekend
Rejoice in God's blessings, ride in the wind

Mountain Air

Bathe in the foggy mist of the mountains as the air—crisp and clean—hosts nature's free spirit. Mountain peaks tower to extremes. Verdant forest scenes lay jagged along the horizon's line. Behold panoramic views that hold breath-taking sights, sounds, smells.

Cool pristine nature of mountain air
Envelops the divine beauty of a forest
Wild animals rustle fallen leaves
Equating spirits of an angelic chorus

A nippy morning stroll through the woods
Finds pastoral inspiration amid nature
Nostrils flare as lungs begin to clear
Affirming intensified senses of rapture

Scent of homemade bread smells heavenly
Remarkably after a walk in the cool, fresh air
Chunks dunked in steaming cappuccino
Donate a creamy, vanilla flavor to the flair

A step outside onto a balcony
Catches a soft breeze tousling the hair
Calm breaths seize the serenity
Welcoming the chilly, crisp mountain air

The view toward the shadowy horizon
Overlooks a crystal-clear mountain lake
Frequent wildlife visitors walk the shoreline
Scampering in midst of a slight wake

Midday siesta beckons the hammock
Where lying down casts eyes skyward
No planes overhead, just blue sky
Where few intermingled clouds drift outward

As time draws nigh to end the day
Deep breaths add pleasure to the scene
The sun settles into twilight
With thoughts of destiny foreseen

Star-studded, moonlit night gatherings
Convene as if under a magic spell
Night owls, birds, wild animals emerge
Conceding to familiar sights and smells

Nature's marvels, nature's scenes
Compile the wildest bucket list
Awe-inspiring natural wonders
Single breaths find hard to resist

Melody amidst mountain air
Drifts with a relaxing chime
It's *breathing the breath of life*
Enchantment—one breath at a time

SEA, SHELLS & SMELLS

Sea, shells, and smells play with your heartstrings. The sea, often fierce, offers a place of serenity. Shells, pearls of the sea, share melodies once held dear. Sulfur smells seep through the air like salty kitchens of sandcastles.

A trip to the beach implies—
Seagulls in flight, crashing waves, sandy toes
Ocean spray in gaping mouths
Tangy sea air infiltrating the nose

A walk on the beach uncovers—
Sandcastles, starfish, sand dollars, seashells
Sea crabs among beds of seagrass
Aromatic scents of salty sea smells

A day at the beach commands—
Scented tanning oil, tan lines
A picnic on a beach blanket
Sea undertow warning signs

A ride along the beach means—
Salty air slapping the face
Sea smells blowing in the wind
Sights filled with surprising grace

A night at the beach offers—
Relaxation embracing the calm
Moonlight reflecting off ocean waves
Lingering smells of sea balm

What is this pungent sea smell?
It's in the air, the sand
Among dead hermit crab shells
Spanning from sea to land

It's the spirit of enthusiasm
Creativity in its prime
Caught up in a gentle breeze
Captivating as a wind chime

It's tiny pearls of inspiration
Scattered along a seashore of decay
Poignant snippets of nature's treasured gifts
Waiting to be found another day

It's the flight of imagination
Inhaling, exhaling with the tide
Something that's to be captured
Filled with emotion seaside

Fantasea

Fabled oceans combine fantasy with tales of the sea where famed mermaids occupy the thoughts of seafarers. Sunlight through a kelp forest lights the charm of sea life nowhere to be found on dry land. Beneath the ocean's surface, wild, wondrous sights lie unscathed.

The sea, volatile yet serene
Holds fast its mystical duty
Emulating, resonating
Mythical, magical beauty

Musings of a sprawling sea
Unlock treasures of yore
Unraveling, revealing
Shipwrecks' elite decor

Such strange, bizarre creatures
Hidden beneath the great wide sea
Shimmering, mirroring
Unquestionable imagery

Sea stars, jellyfish, flatworms
Along the seafloor intertwine
Infusing, captivating
Luminous color by design

Crystal-clear shallows, vast briny depths
Astonish with uplifting insights
Mindboggling, hypnotizing
Thrilling alien highlights

Deepwater sponges, sea anemones
Emit such intricate hues of delight
Bioluminescing, radiating
Eye-striking varying degrees of light

Thoughts of enchanting mermaids
Evoke tales of the southernmost key
Whispering, relinquishing
Enchanted secrets of the deep blue sea

Open sea, daunting yet tranquil
Transfixes your inmost feelings
Generating, emphasizing
Surreal, intense mental paintings

A Walk Along the Beach

Living fast-paced leaves little time alone or with a loved one. When meditative music shifts to peaceful ocean sounds, serious thought processes turn to the sea. To relax, welcome peace with a walk along the beach as you inhale the salty air with deep breaths.

Radiance on the horizon
Broadcasts day is about to begin
Sending sunbeams of golden warmth
To soothe, visibly gild the skin

Sunbeams reflect on the water
Mirroring synthetic jewels
With prismatic colors arching
Inside raindrops like cultured pearls

Noonday scorching, sweltering heat
Offers the darkest, perfect tan
As spilling waves erase footprints
Where sandpipers once swiftly ran

Breathtaking views of sandy beaches
Stretch outward miles upon miles
Where sandcastles' unique creations
Generate smiles upon smiles

Summer evenings, moonlit nights
Flaunt stars for strollers to abide
Lovers walk lonely beaches
Staying close, in step side by side

On daily walks, what are your expectations? Do you presume to encounter amazing sights along with soothing sounds? Think, too, of the smells. Each inhaled breath captures pleasing aromas or those from former lives decayed. Plants breathe. Animals breathe. Sea urchins breathe. Insects breathe. It is the art of breathing that sustains life. Experience Mother Nature's elements with your physical body, emotions, and inner spirit. Expect the unexpected. Imagine awesome!

Majestic Breath

Do you have a daily walk and talk with Mother Nature?

WALK WITH NATURE

Walking. Exercise meant to be
Just counting steps, one, two, then three
Like clockwork, daily routine
Missing out on every scene

I walked, then I walked some more
Examining Mother Nature's floor
Beds of leaves where nature crept
Nests in trees where birdies slept

A nature walk—
It's eye-opening. It's spellbinding.
It's outdoors. It's nature's floors.

Thought for a New Day: *Walk among the wonders of nature opening your heart, mind, and soul to a world of enlightenment. Let nature be your soulmate!*

There are no excuses for missing out on the excitement
or tranquility of Mother Nature!
Sunshine is delicious, rain is refreshing, wind braces us up,
snow is exhilarating; there is really no such thing as bad
weather, only different kinds of good weather.
—John Ruskin (Writer, Philosopher, Art Critic, 1819–1900

SMELL THE RAIN

Rain dances many rhythms—drizzle to sprinkle, steady flow to downpour. Raindrops fall with grace or flash dance with thunder. With an approaching rainstorm, a sweet, pungent smell rises from its earthly embrace. That's when "It smells like rain!"

With day's first light
A bracing essence drifts by
As sunbeams peep
From behind clouds in the sky

Sense of a looming storm
Tickles the nostrils, then departs
But have you ever stopped
To smell rain before it starts?

Ah! Nothing like the aroma
Of fresh-baked homemade bread
Or that distinct powerful scent
Warm cinnamon rolls spread!

Such succulent senses
Can dull any pain
But have you ever stopped
To smell morning rain?

Peace abides in the meadow
'Til twilight in the countryside
Where wet spicy fragrances
Of newly-cut timbers abide

Subtle, soothing perfumes
The colorful wildflowers yield
But have you ever stopped
To smell rain in a grassy field?

Gray skies, stormy days
May sense of the forlorn
When the storm passes
A colorful hue is born

A bold rainbow arches
O'er a weather vane
But have you ever stopped
To smell lashing rain?

A farm road embraces
An afternoon shower
As dusty mist bathes
Each tree, every flower

Within a few moments
Freshness of senses is bestowed
But have you ever stopped
To smell rain on a dusty road?

Breathe in the rain smells
Part of Mother Nature's domain
Dance in the puddles
Left behind by the pouring rain

When the forecast is rainfall
Break away from daily routines
Let the rhythm of falling rain
Compose a song of tranquil scenes

Around the Campfire

As sparks shoot skyward, the campfire's embers mingle with the twinkling stars. Phantom shadows casting ghostly resonances lead to spooky tales, spine-chilling as the night air. A hoot owl shatters thoughts as you roast a marshmallow over the open fire.

Nothing like the burning smell
Of a cozy sizzling fire
As amber-glowing embers
Displace any chilling ire

Cups of rich piping hot cocoa
Ease bitterness of the cold
When vapor rises to the nostrils
On downward deep into the soul

Simple auras of nature
Sentimental thoughts aspire
Wintry pine needles, pine cones
Sizzle, snap, pop in the fire

Old favorite campfire songs
Echo smiles, oodles of laughter
Snuggling during ghost stories
Renew memories thereafter

In the fairy-tale hour of midnight
No stronger aura doth inspire
Than riveting phantom spirits
Circling the blazing open campfire

FESTIVE FÊTE

Heralding each change in season are sights and sounds of craft fairs. The best part is the aromatic smells. Outdoor tables feature local well-crafted items. Choices range from antiques, handmade pottery, home-cooked foods to the most unusual gifts imaginable.

Spring, summer, fall, even winter
Inspire seasonal local bazaars
White elephant rooms offer items
Like out-of-tune broken guitars

Rave musicians, native artists
Venture forth nearby, far and wide
Camaraderie, festive cheer
Encircle arts and crafts outside

Bounties of comforting soul foods
Herald accolades to each chef
Brioche, chocolates, delicacies
Create competition for a ref

Friends, as well as total strangers
Greet each other by the hand
No one goes without attention
And everyone loves the band

Cuisine of the grand Festive Fête
Finds every crumb taste-tested
Whiffs of tempting, tantalizing eats
Leave nary a morsel wasted

Ghosts, Spirits & Cinnamon

Eerie atmospheres connect to ghost stories and spirits. Cinnamon smells announce fresh, homemade treats or a hot toddy ready to warm chilled bones. Tales circulate when the cinnamon smell declares a visit of a loved one straight from the spirit world.

Bare trees donned with snow-white hoarfrost
Leave gray-white berries in plain view
Gracing the boughs like sizeable pearls

Chestnuts roasting on an open fire
Invite closeness within its coziness
Warming as a ghost story unfurls

Naked branches upon gray backdrops
Reveal spirits of emptiness
Deepening one's imagination

Tinkling icicles breaking silence
Capture winter's austere presence
Opening gates of fascination

Tales of phantom spirits' ghastly presence
Propel chills right through to the bone
Urging all near to jump up and scream

Cups of homemade piping hot spiced tea
Boast stirrers of stick cinnamon
Calming the air of an eerie scene

Fragrance of bayberry, cinnamon
Spicy, woodsy, subtlety sweet
Filters all around market town

Freshly fallen snow kisses the earth
Covering the December fields
Like a blanket of white fluffy down

Children slipping and sliding on icy ground
Frolicking and playing, throwing snowballs
Fill the air with cheers and roaring laughter

Sounds of melodious harps and chimes
Add a magical spice to the scene
Yesterday, today, and hereafter

Scented candles along the mantle
Flicker 'til burned all the way down
Meant for good fortune in the New Year

Such are ghosts, spirits, and cinnamon
Shared with friends, family, loved ones
In the forefront of holiday cheer

Holiday Aromatic Classics

Holiday whiffs tickle the nose along busy sidewalks where everything glows. Shoppers teem with joy, which dims chaos of the season. Bundle up outside in wintry weather or cuddle up in front of a cozy fireplace where classic scents inspire each moment.

Whimsical gingerbread houses
Adorned with jelly beans and candy canes
Host shingles of cinnamon-flavored gum
As red licorice ropes frame window panes

Holiday classic cookie bliss
Turned into absolute kitchen madness
Sends haphazard wisps of flour-sugar mix
Twirling into billowy mounds of sweetness

Balsam fir's spirited pine needle fragrance
Rekindled by long-lasting memories
Brings the brisk smell of the outdoors inside
Competing with candle scents of homespun candies

Homemade spicy apple cider
Highlighted by studded oranges with cloves
Simmers in a crockpot for many hours
Welcoming home holiday guests by the droves

Stir rods of soft peppermint twists
Bundled with shiny silvery ribbons
Await their placement in hot cider mugs
To activate warming, comforting visions

Maple pecan, fresh apple, spiced pumpkin pies
Home-baked with love until a golden affair
Rouse desire in anticipation
As scents drift playfully in midair

Brown sugar-glazed sweet potatoes
Simply mashed, souffléd like Grandma used to do
Demand multiple replies when ready
"Hallelujah! Thank you! Thank you! Thank you!"

Smoky comfort of crackling logs
Stacked one on top of another
Invite coziness around the fireplace
Embracing loved ones, sister and brother

Breaths of those holiday classics
Aromatic scents of freshness to share
Waft over, around, through the streets
Bringing those you love together with flair

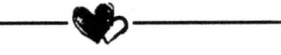

Have you noticed Mother Nature boasts fragrant perfumes? The aura of a conifer forest, the earthy aroma of wet soil, and the fresh scent of a rippling stream energize the inner spirit. Even frankincense and myrrh support tranquility. An odor, whether slight or powerful, exists with every breath you take. Degrees of smell await your response. Note unique fragrances for bittersweet is the breath of life, nonetheless surprising and interesting!

Aromatic Airs

What do the thorns of a rose reveal?

FRAGRANT ROSE

A rose is a rose, what do I perceive?
Fragrant fragility right before me
Velvety petals tender to the touch
Unknowingly of beauty loved so much

I smelled the rose, absorbed its loveliness
Touched its petals, felt its comfortness
Reached down for one, pricked by a thorn
Prompted swiftly it hurt same as scorn

The thorny rose—
It lives. It dies.
It wiles. It reconciles.

Thought for a New Day: *The breath of life brings clarity into a new day with rekindled insights into daily precious moments. Restate your urges!*

Somethin's Cookin'

The best of times begot magic of the kitchen. Tasks around the stove began at sunup, infusing the entire house with tempting aromas. When unexpected folk showed up, fast food involved preparing extra servings in a hurry.

The screen door slams without any mention
As small feet scamper into the kitchen
"What are you doing, Daddy," someone cries
"Whiffs of somethin' cookin' have spread outside"

"What does it smell like? Does it tickle your wee nose?
It's something from the yard where fresh fruit grows
It's tangy, it's sweet, eaten any time you please
Can be served with ice cream, sharp cheddar cheese!"

"Oh, Daddy, you're so silly," she replies
"I know what's cookin'—hot apple pies
Mama baked them when she was at home
You've taken over now that she's gone"

Somethin's cookin' other than the pies
A hardy meal is the big surprise
"What's for dinner, Daddy?" she pleaded
"Food, good food," though he quickly conceded

Hearty hickory-smoked country ham
Center place on dinner's program
Collard greens, yams, corn on the cob
Compete with apple pies as high nob

No meal is a meal without cornbread
Cracklin', pone, muffins declare 'nuff said
But wait! There's classic Southern and Southern light
Ready for dunkin' in buttermilk at night

Table's all ready, each dish in its place
Pies set aside in their own marked space
Pungent smells of the treat that lies ahead
Tempt tiny appetites like fresh bread

Despite many pleas, pies stay only within sight
For they will be served after dinner tonight
With company coming, Aunt Sue and Uncle Wade
Whopping pitchers of iced tea need to be made

The screen door slams with the same refrain
As tiny little feet return outside again
Running, racing, playing really hard
With the smell of those pies lingering in the yard

ROCKING CHAIR MOTION

Memories of watching Grandma in that dear old rocking chair emulate a most important memory—carefree, relaxing moments. Today, yours may be a porch rocking chair. Spend time surrounded by fresh breaths of morning or night air.

The rhythmic movement of life
Imitates a rocking chair in motion
Moving forward and backward
Cautiously with conditioned emotion

Life's continuous patterns
Remain subconscious, keenly alive
Pledging freedom through wholeness
Within a willingness to survive

Busyness as well as business
Become routine, at times collide
Leaving little time for self
To unwind from the inside

Mimicking the rocking chair
Forward, then backward, life rocks
Stabilizing daily walks
Amid many stumbling blocks

A matter of mere balance
Interprets the day, also the night
Exiling daily stresses
In a breath of absolute delight

Pure joy of discovery
Lies amid a flash of frustration
Bringing breathless calls to life
Within instant gratification

An element of elegance
Sets the stage for a graceful scene
Defining moments of tranquility
As soft as candlelight and fine cuisine

Stretching, yawning upon wakening
Trigger fresh breaths of morning air
Relaxing earlier worries away
Like motion of the rocking chair

In the corner of your eye
The rocking chair is in view
Waiting to be in motion
When toils of the day are through

LIFE SMELLS BETTER WITHOUT TELEVISION

Television offers cooking and sports channels along with reality TV shows. But, the senses of smell, taste, and touch are behind the scenes. You may have a clear image of a waterfall and hear its thunderous roar. Lost is feeling the mist as it crashes into the pool below.

Television grips center stage
Taking hold of senses like caffeine
News broadcasts, sports, reality TV
Project a rather common scene

With cable TV and internet out
Life takes on a different view
A strange sense of euphoria exists
Sweeping quite surprisingly through

With the kitchen now the ideal hub
Aromatic pleasures hold the resolve
What tempting delicacy awaits?
That's the lingering problem to solve!

Aromas of mouthwatering treats
Capture the pickiest appetites
Why live in someone else's reality
When you can savor the tasty bites?

The air smells enticingly better
Distant from the TV screen
Carefree talk at the dinner table
Projects an uncommon scene

Who did what, when, how in preparation
Become bragging rights of the hour
Time passes by exceedingly fast
With smiles, laughter being the power

Time after a filling, robust meal
Demands a leisurely stroll
Beats "parking" in front of the TV
Where just sittin' takes its toll

Opening the door welcomes fresh air
Unwanted thoughts quickly disappear
Sights, sounds, even smells of the outdoors
Incite joy, even a happy tear

Once outside conversation continues
Informal talk is the best chatter
If I were . . . if you could . . . if we only . . .
Leads to solving day's most urgent matter

Life smells better, *is* better
Without television in the way
Hearken to the call outside
Breathe deeply, enjoy nature's buffet!

MOTHER NATURE'S BUFFETS

Buds and blossoms flaunt a rainbow of colors, a specialty of design by Mother Nature. Pick your own flowers; create your own nature bouquet. Bedeck a vase or basket with a dazzling display of subtle shades of splendor.

Sweet Azaleas of springtime
Boast perfumes flowing like fountains
Along the eastern coastal shores
Through the Appalachian Mountains

Aphrodite blossoms in summer
Bring joy, love, peace in harmony
Adding the fragrances of rose oils
Often to scenes of matrimony

Climbing Sweet Autumn Clematis
Cascades white starry flowers
Leaving intensely fragrant scents
Lingering minutes to hours

Winter's American witch hazel
Adds richness to a bleak season
Donning tables with scented flowers
Within arrays for any reason

No heartless, plastic flowers
Line Mother Nature's aromatic table
Just intoxicating, bold "buffets"—
Bountiful, elegantly available

DELICATE ALBA ROSE

You should be familiar with the expression "a rose is a rose." Each poetic mention focuses on the loveliness the rose discloses. As Shakespeare penned: Would a rose by any other name remain a rose? It would be the same symbol of love, only its name would be different.

Pure beauty of an Alba rose
Red color of a fragile nature
Implies simplicity though complex
Within a soft, fleshy texture

Fragrance of the elegant rose
Evocative perfume of pleasure
Hangs midair waiting to be inhaled
As nature's redolent treasure

Alluring attar of the rose
Entices a flower bee after rain
Sips of nature's fragrant liquid
Nourishes until he's off again

Carefully plucking one by one
Petals are delicately laid
Being mindful of prickly thorns
While forming a flawless cascade

Tempting perfume of the rose
Permeates the soul of all mankind
Forgives by instinctive nature
Healing the heart, calming the mind

Are you becoming more aware of nature's occurrences? Mother Nature's strong beat beckons the likeness of musical chords. The elements of nature—earth, water, wind, fire—are synchronized within time and space. Whether in your kitchen gazing out the window, outside smelling the roses, or leisurely sitting in your porch rocking chair, you are always in sync with Mother Nature. Life moves on, following the natural cycles of nature.

Rhythmic Cycles

How have you heard, seen, smelled, tasted, or felt nature's rhythm?

NATURE'S RHYTHM

Reclining upon earth's damp blanket
Mother Nature posed a sense of calm
I breathed deeply, yielding a soft sigh
As a ladybug tickled my arm

A clean earthy fragrance filled the air
As colors of a rainbow burst
For a rain shower not long before
Rhythmically quenched nature's thirst

Nature's spirit—
It's elemental. It's fundamental.
It's energy. It's synergy.

Thought for a New Day: *Anticipate tomorrow with slow, rhythmic movements of breathing, syncing nature's rhythm with your heartbeat. Make each breath count!*

ONE BREATH AT A TIME

Busy, busy, busy! Hurry, hurry, hurry! Frantically you move about in a daze with rapid, shallow breaths. Life is filled to the brim with many demands. Hectic has become life when failure to slow down prevents breathing deeply, taking life one breath at a time.

You enter this world
Startled as you gasp
This first breath of life
Nothing can surpass

At life's first breath
You are in love's zone
Beloved who are near
Wait to bring you home

Contentment in relief
Incites a deep sigh
Strong arms gently cradle
Your body brought nigh

Emotions soar indeed
Tears of joy are shed
Thoughts shift to changes
What lies ahead

Within only a few minutes
Perhaps an hour or so
Recognition is imminent
Of someone you'll soon know

As the clock ticks, time passes
Whether sleeping or awake
Unconsciously, naturally
Life is every breath you take

You receive each deep breath
This air that you breathe
Good-humored with joy
Ill-tempered as you seethe

Breathing comes naturally
Without labor or thought
Inhaling in rhythmic time
With each new breath sought

Spirit of your soul
Guides your every breath
Inhaling, exhaling
Stopping only at death

Find your unique rhythm
Effortlessly to achieve
Inhaling deeply to heal
Exhaling to relieve

Whether gasp or sigh
Slow or double-time
Take life as it is—
One breath at a time!

Angel's Sigh

Have you felt an angel looking over your shoulder or in your presence when you sought comfort? Soft whispers and signs around you—white feathers, pennies, butterflies, robins, rainbows, dreams, gleams of light—leave an aura of an angel's presence.

An angel peers down
Breathing a heartfelt sigh
Far below two lovers
Prepare their good-bye

One remains at home
The other's off to war
Neither wants separation
Both want life as before

Face to face they stand
Only a breath apart
Solemn is the scene
For they are one of heart

The concern in her face
Is of solitude, fear
So tender his caress
Wiping away a tear

As the final moment
Of departure nears
A lone flicker of light
Suddenly appears

Wispy breaths brush
Each tenderly on the cheek
"Did you feel that?" she asks
In a voice soft and meek

The spirit hugs both
As leaving draws nigh
They adoringly embrace
Grateful for the angel's sigh

ALL IN A SINGLE BREATH

Breath is the air you breathe. Breadth is desire governed by choices. Amidst an unpleasant aroma, you elect to hold your breath. In the mountains, you breathe deeply the cool, crisp air. For both, the breadth is how long you feel each is significant.

Breathe the breath of life
Standing in the sunlight
Inhaling, exhaling true freedom
With slight effort, no fight

Understand the breadth
Of choices within each hour
Inhaling deep or shallow
Feel the real power

Commit to a morning walk
Where smells of morning remain
Inhale, exhale with thoughts
Some are rich, others plain

Relax in the night air
Notice a windy chill
Inhaling, exhaling the coolness
All of free will

Inhale, exhale seizing every single moment.
Life is about choices, all in a single breath.

OUR LAST BREATH (TOGETHER)

Togetherness shares morning smiles along with goodbye kisses. At the end of the day, comfort is reaffirmed as you walk alongside Mother Nature. One in mind, one in spirit, one in love, you share the same dreams until your last breath together.

Our life together is one—
One of heart, one of mind
With undying spirit
Always open, ne'er confined

Contented moments as one—
Side by side, in each other's arms
To caress, to be caressed,
Duly faithful throughout life's storms

Inner thoughts become one—
Feeling what each other feels
In tune to every moment
Without remorse, without frills

We play always as one—
Both take part on center stage
Counting each precious moment
During our changes in age

It is indeed no wonder—
We remain one forever
From first kiss to last kiss
Our last breath together

TAKE A DEEP BREATH!

A new awareness of the inner self comes with the art of deep breathing. With your eyes closed or open, gradual deep breaths stimulate your senses. Each exhaled breath releases tension as the body relaxes. What is in front of your eyes becomes sharper.

What do you do when sadness strikes—
Look to family, seek friends perhaps?
Find a place of solace in solitude?

There is joy in being alive
No need to forego life's true meaning
Wiling away hours in a somber mood

Joy and sadness go hand in hand—
One finds the other, clearly unplanned
Undoubtedly heart to heart, soul to soul

Deep breaths in the natural world
Decrease stress, deepening insight
Expanding consciousness beyond control

Take this advice under your wing—
Restore energy, sense inner peace
Take a deep breath relishing the relief

Step outside, look up to the sky
Delight in marvels before your eyes
Strengthen the awareness of your belief

What is the most significant aspect of life that's taken for granted? Breathing—for breath IS life! The art of breathing is a remarkably natural occurrence, effortless. You live in your cultural, traditional, spiritual self while the entire universe is in perfect rhythm with the breath of life. With that thought in mind, the beat of life goes on, one breath at a time, always in sync with Mother Nature.

Easily Emphatic

When have you paid attention to your breath of life?

BREATH OF LIFE

I breathe the breath of life
Without much thought and little effort
It comes naturally
Yielding little or no discomfort

Mother Nature's breaths
Take my breath away every hour
From caressing winds
To the budding of a flower

Breath of life—
It's inhaling. It's exhaling.
It's rhythmic. It's emphatic.

Thought for a New Day: *Breathe deeply in silent meditation to enhance aromas and flavors ever-present in the world around you. Capture the essence!*

~ Spirit in Nature! ~

As the natural world awakens, wonder begins! Early morn brings forth fresh sights within sounds intermingled with raw smells of earth. Crackling of dried leaves underfoot breaks through the silence along with songs of birds.

On cool mornings, little clouds of fog appear with each exhaled breath. Watching sunbeams glance off dew-laden foliage spins you around to catch every beam. The scurrying of tiny critters is startling as they hurry back into their secure havens.

Enjoy fantasy moments in reality:
Dance with spirits, hold hands with Mother Nature!

SENSE THE SPIRIT!

Mother Nature's spirit captures your soul within purple scenery. Hold on to its power with a warm heart as you breathe each single breath of life. A comforting spirit heals, erases, and relieves distress, if only for a moment.

A spirit exists among wildlife
Taking charge cougar style
Of graceful movement, a guiding light
Enduring, versatile

Unlike the cougar
Rarely heard, seldom seen
This spirit's everywhere
Behind every scene

Outdoor flowering essence
Intensifies when near it
Goddesses of raw beauty
Paint nature a free spirit

Senses are keener
Inviting deeper breaths
Summoning up feelings
From magical depths

Life's incredible collage
So close you can't miss it
Landscapes, colors, creatures
Of unique healing spirit

Trails of raw inspiration
Pure as a psalm
Appear sunlit or subdued
Stormy or calm

The power of spirit
Thrives on the unexpected
Be ready, willing, on-call
Alert and connected

Experience Life! *Go forth. Sense the spirit!*

Nature always wears the colors of the spirit.
— Ralph Waldo Emerson (Essayist, 1803–1882)

Life is full of beauty. Notice it. Notice the bumble bee,
the small child, and the smiling faces.
Smell the rain and feel the wind. Live your life
to the fullest potential, and fight for your dreams.
— Ashley Smith (Author, b. 1978)

Savor Life to Its Fullest

*With heart and soul
Conquer life at its finest
Enjoy the thrill of it all—
Savor life to its fullest!*

Lesson from Catnip

*Favor the finer flavors of life—
All-natural and fundamental!*

TIME ENOUGH

"I just don't have enough time!" Sound familiar? Enough time for what— to exercise, cook, clean, dream? Are you too busy, too tired? Time is relative to everything you do. Recognizing priority uncovers more time than you can imagine.

What is the essence of life?
Is it living for the moment
Loving for a lifetime or
Existing to be affluent?

If it is living for the moment
The slightest instant must count
Recognizing each single moment
Allows blessings to surmount

Since the moments are precious
Loving for a lifetime is priceless
Fulfilling life's dreams, passions
With promises seemingly timeless

If it is happiness your heart desires
Don't let affluence leave you blind
Enjoying the simple pleasures of life
Is what's inherent to mankind

Capture the intent in a moment
Whether easy or tough
It's *savoring life to its fullest*
For there is time enough!

Life's Finer Moments

Seasons occur when we share with and care for those we love. The groundwork for days ahead involves accepting and forgiving. Memory provides flashbacks of the finer moments better remembered when filled with love.

Life's finer moments
Altogether duty-free
From smiles to laughter
Never warrant any fee

Reflections in a mirror
Entice making faces for fun
One brings about another
With laughter never outdone

Butterfly wispy wings
Softly brush the skin
To quickly fly away
Adrift in the wind

Tiny crystals of dew
Adorn morning roses
Whilst the sweet aroma
Tickles little noses

Outdoors eagerly beckons
Running, hiking up a hill
With country horseback riding
Adding vigor to the thrill

Sharp-tailed wading sandpipers
Group together along the beach
Collectors gather seashells
The tide deposits within reach

Dark shadows of twilight
Appear as phantoms of the night
Holding a loved one's hand
Eliminates all fear or fright

A newborn baby's cry
Brings tension amid joy
With tears of happiness
No matter girl or boy

Special time with family
Cites feelings in expressive talk
Renewing strength to carry on
Within, throughout life's daily walk

Grandmother's best sweater
Being hugged under the nose
Smells of fresh-cut lilacs
ithin memory that glows

Life's finer moments
Lay within your midst
Do you have any
To add to the list?

BEARS, BEES & STINGS

If the bee didn't love nectar, the flowers wouldn't become pollinated—thus, life could be bitter without honey. The bear bites; the bee stings. So goes life as emotional upsets turn the pages of the most romantic novel.

Attuned to the winter cold
Hibernation's natural to a bear
With shorter days, longer nights
Sleeping becomes the primary affair

Flight of the bee during winter
Decreases protectively
Harboring the queen is the goal
Clustering collectively

Sentiments of a winter season
Affirm human nature's lassitude
Reflections mirror past to present
Creating a melancholy mood

The early days of springtime
Catch bees at work on the crocus
With the snow at last melting
Activity is the focus

New life buzzing all around
Finds everyone busy as the bee
Making plans, meeting demands
Go about as far as one can see

Nature in its own pristine beauty
Flourishes after winter's thaw
Prickly, bristly thorns, sharp spiny things
Emerge clothed in springtime's awe

The bear awakens with hunger
While the bee strikes with its stinger
Freshness, newness of life abounds
As winter memories linger

Springtime's awe-inspiring insects
Reside within each blade of grass
Nature's gripping creepie crawlies
Spread whimsical wings as they pass

Lovers stroll along forest paths
Inhaling the newness nature brings
Spring announces love's presence
Even within emotional stings

At Your Fingertips

Life overflows with treasures, visible and vague. Many of Mother Nature's riches represent natural gems without the expensive price tag. They enrich the mind, heart, and soul. Abundances of this quality outshine things you can buy or sell.

Life's small treasures frankly go unnoticed
It's so easy to let little things slip
Some pass by unrecognized or ignored
When they are right there at your fingertips

Daily observance of natural surroundings
Reveals riches sitting right under your nose
A word of encouragement or simply a smile
Waits to be esteemed before it quickly goes

Holding an elder's hand while crossing the street
Soothingly wiping a tear from a child's eye—
Precious moments that need to be understood
For too soon it will be time to say good-bye

The sunrise in its dawning glory
The sunset with its soft amber glow
Embellish plush meadows, green hillsides
Where nature's bounties quietly flow

Why do you worry about tomorrow
When there is so much to live for today?
Think about the blessings each day bestows
Hold them in your heart to help guide the way

All of nature's delightful wonders
Embrace feelings hard to impart
Ready, willing to ease the pain
Of a lost loved one or broken heart

Look around, forward, never backward
Examine the panoramic view
What's to your left is not to your right
Even the middle's different too

Whether looking upward or downward
There is always something new
Keep joy in your heart, a smile on your face
Goodness is always in view

Don't let any of life's small treasures go unnoticed
Be watchful of each little thing before it slips
None should pass by unrecognized, ignored
When it is right there at your fingertips

SAVORING THE RAIN

Springtime showers offer rainfall as a precursor to buds and blossoms. Summer rains are sudden reliefs from the heat. An autumn shower adds sparkle to the season's color changes. During the winter, frozen rain forms mosaics in the ice and snow.

Existing is a tingle of pain
In standing under lashing rain
Following each sting comes relief
Even if only openly brief

Slivers of light sweep across the sky
As smoky clouds drift slowly by
Casual movements leisurely bring
Peace from each perpetual sting

Thunder rumbles as a moving train
Signaling the next sheaf of rain
Shelter is sought in a quaint café
Far from torrential dismay

Tempting sights of chocolate toffee
Sink in steaming mugs of coffee
Each sip takes away innermost chills
With the rain pounding windowsills

Rain pierces the air like glass sheets
'Til the storm finally retreats
So, where is joy within the pain?
It's all about savoring the rain!

What does savor mean? Enjoy something undeniably without question! Throughout life, emotions surface from sighs to outcries. No two happenings are the same, nor are their emotional reactions. Think of a kaleidoscope. With each rotation, glass cells inside twist and turn resulting in an ever-changing view. That's life—some days excite, some bite, some cling, some sting. When emotions blur, shift focus to the good things you savor in life.

Sentiments of Emotion

What wonders of nature cause your emotions to surge?

SURGING EMOTIONS

Witness the opening of morning glories
Hear the hummingbird with its gentle whistle
Listen to the wind whispering to the trees
Watch the seed dispersal of the milk thistle

Dance joyfully to the rhythm of nature's spirit
Yield to nature's mindful moments with a simple sigh
Surge with emotion as you see it, hear it, feel it
Become lost in the mystery of the dragonfly

Emotion—
It's sad. It's glad.
It's strong. It belongs.

Thought for a New Day: *Absorb everything you see, hear, and feel to their fullest; the rewards are priceless. State your claims!*

MYSTICAL & MAGICAL

Within mystical allure may lie a bit of magic. In the land of the mysterious, questions arise. The answers are hard to define within the spoken or written word, nor is it possible to fully explain them. These are the miracles.

Watch raindrops dance across a flower
Catch a ray of sun, feel its power
Brush windswept hair from across your face
Feel elegance of Chantilly lace

Bathe in watercolors of sunrises
Open your eyes to all the surprises
Cherish the twilight, dusk or dawn
Hail mystic beauty hours doth spawn

Grab a softball, toss it with a child
Tickle a baby, watch them smile
Save a caterpillar, let it be
Laud butterfly wings soon you'll see

Lay your head upon someone's chest
Feel each heartbeat as you rest
Cry when time to be parted
Let tears refresh the love imparted

Pause when wistful sounds draw nigh
Breathe softly a soulful sigh
Listen to birds sing off key
Magic through your veins flows free

Nature's Calendar

An ordinary day becomes passionate when exposed to the flair amongst the flavor of the outdoors. Challenge yourself to notice nature's surprises from month to month. Seek the newness with each turn of the calendar's page.

Nature's calendar unfolds natural wonder
As every month sets renowned visions asunder

January brings ice palaces and snow
With flora lying dormant underneath
February stirs cold depths of winter
Echoing sounds of cha-chattering teeth

March embraces gusty winds
Cutting right to the bone
With April close at hand
Bringing spring showers home

Cherry blossoms erupt in May
Flaunting treasuries of lush leafy trees
June yields rich succulent flora
Under temperatures of top degrees

July incites intense heat
As celebrations cross the land
Hot August brings waving fields
Those amber golden grains command

September invites autumn harvest time
Shorter days, falling leaves, changing landscapes
Whilst October's yellows, oranges, burnt reds
Offer brilliantly spirited debates

November notes Thanksgiving
Cornucopias, overfilled and sublime
Frigid December ends the year
With traditional Yule logs at Christmas time

So much waiting to be embraced
Within the twelve months of the year
Fleeting moments to be captured
Calling out daily "over here"

Over here, over there, everywhere
Impossible to catch them all
Remain in tune, in sync, enthralled
Don't miss the simple natural call

Open Sky

The sky is a cosmic canvas. A Midwestern thunderstorm reveals its special masterpiece whereas a desert sky exposes amazing stars in its night sky. Wherever you go, an open sky tests your imagination with uncluttered, unscathed, visceral beauty.

Love for life brings joyousness
The moment it has begun
Power from which all arises
Under the moon, under the sun

First sight of morning light
Illuminates a wide-open sky
Thoughts render mysticism
As a billowing cloud passes by

Sheer splendor of existence
Hidden if walking through pain
Overtly resurfaces
After energizing rain

Impressiveness is powerful
After the noon hour has passed
Skies invite a heartfelt glare
Baring more than anyone asked

A flirting breeze at sundown
Refreshes as two hearts meet
Silences command wonder
Loneliness dares to compete

Desire stretches into the twilight
Where naught has gone awry
Letting go, succumbing to love
Beneath an open sky

Wonders of the universe
Erupt in breathtaking night skies
Falling stars in their brilliance
Surrender within intrinsic sighs

Love, life, togetherness
Profess eternal pleasure
Faces of love remain
Beyond time, place, or measure!

Evanescent Twilight

Soft, shadowy hues of twilight induce tranquility. Time seems to stand motionless, thoughts drift away to a magical place, worry becomes a thing of the past. Glimmering silver essences at twilight embody remnants of an enchanting daydream.

Between dawn and sunrise
When daybreak abandons night's chill
The sun barely visible
Ascends in slow motion until . . .

Sunlight scatters along the horizon
Where clouds catch the first rays of dawn
Erupting into a blaze of color
Only Heaven could possibly spawn

Standing on the edge of silence
A sense of calm penetrates the soul
Hovering between darkness and light
Sheer magnificence to behold

Between sunset and dusk
Day's last light seems to stand still
The sun barely visible
Descends in slow motion until . . .

Intense color splashes across the horizon
Where the sky catches the sun's last rays
Illuminating a thin veil of haziness
Below the clouds that are now ablaze

Witnessing such magnificence
Ignites emotion in the soul
Tears of rendered ecstasy well up
As sentiments willingly extol

Between dusk and dawn
Where time seemingly stands still
The sun no longer visible
Retains its brilliance until . . .

A silhouetted figure lost and alone
Against the pending backdrop of night
Grasps the last red-orange rays of the sun
Fervently kissing the day's twilight

With radiant images now past
The world becomes shrouded in gray
Whilst the twinkling of night's first stars
Engulfs the glories of the day

EDGE OF CREATION

Being on the edge may find you in a precarious situation. You are almost there, but teeter between excitement and risk. Standing on the edge of a cliff presents a different viewpoint. There you are on the edge of creation with certainty.

Surrounded by the stillness
Of warm earthen desert scenes
Lustrous golden-brown hues
Engulf mud-sculptured ravines

Mysterious etchings
Steer thoughts to eras past
Stirring desire to translate
The century, the year cast

Self-guided natural trails
Drop into steep rugged canyons
Snaking their way back up again
Changing like chameleons

Dazzling spectacles of color
Adorn rocky canyon walls
Reflecting warm desert light
Reminiscent of gilded halls

Massive rocky palisades
Stand firm on the edge of creation
Formidable in every respect
Breathless, beyond imagination

Do you feel you have ever been in the world of fantasy? Fantasized moments resemble the mystical, magical dragon. Along with things of a mystical and magical nature also arises the mythical Mermaid of the sea. Mermaids, along with the elusive dragon, may change over time in magical quality—unsurpassed in mysticism. Whether reality or fantasy, such vivid occurrences are to be treasured as mystical, magical days of pure joy.

Mystical & Magical

What myths, magic, or mysticism have you encountered lately?

MYTHS, MAGIC & MYSTICISM

Two sides to a story always exist
Yet in nature one will often find three
Nature *myths* account for the shapes of plants
Handling of bird nests, monsters of the sea

Nature's *magic* makes everything okay
Calms a moment, heals the heart, soothes the soul
While *mysticism* frames nature's spirit
Keeping mind and body under control

Myths, magic & mysticism . . .
They're ever-present. Often reticent.
They're overstated. Sometimes underestimated.

Thought for a New Day: *Remain empowered regardless of the day's appearance; look beyond the clouds toward the joy of life. Feel the magic!*

SOMETIMES LIFE IS LONELY

Time alone is welcomed via a walk with Mother Nature or at the seashore creating oneness with the ocean. Loneliness has little to do with being alone. Life with nature has a strange way of feeding your senses when you need nourishment.

Loneliness may come from sorrow
As tears gush forth like pouring rain
With a nature walk alone being welcomed
When nothing else surprisingly eases the pain

Aloneness with nature is a blessing
Away from the hectic tumults of life
Banishing the sights, sounds, or signs
Of confusion, discontent, strife

Alone could be resourceful
Inspiring a relaxed thought
Perhaps a laugh with Mother Nature
Instead of feelings yielding distraught

Inspiration nesting in one's mind
Awakens amid calm meditation
Renewing life's spiritual strength
While resting upon nature's foundation

Sometimes life is lonely, so sad
Garnering frowns of fear or dread
Seek out times being alone with nature
Employ smiling thoughts and laughter instead

Love's Presence

Awakening from winter's sleep, Mother Nature bursts forth in song as she bids ashen tones goodbye. Spirits renew love's aura as it fills the air, being swept along by gentle breezes. Fiery sunrises, flaming sunsets mirror warm hues of wood fires.

Smell of newly mown grass
Bears breaths of new beginnings
Birthing, budding, blossoming
All within their own innings

Soft wispy breath of spring
In its light of innocence
Suffuses the meadows
With a hint of tenderness

Nature's arms embrace
Morning warmth of the sun
When buds to blossoms
Awaken with the dawn

Within each winter's wake up
The fields, the forests come alive
Like seen in fairy tales
Green flora, new fauna arrive

Robins as first sign of spring
Whether wives' tale or fact
Perched on apple tree branches
Invite rare eye contact

Fanciful hummingbirds
Hovering soul-scorching bliss
Blur mistily their wings
Igniting sweet nectar's kiss

Butterflies' dainty wings
Fluttering a gentle breeze
Capture graceful whispers
Caressing all they please

Lovers conscientiously stroll
Arm in arm, hand in hand
Admiring elegant wonders
Within splendor of the land

Beauty of springtime
Void of the bitter cold
Propels love's presence
Deep down into the soul

For the Love of You

Whether sunny skies or rainy days, love's presence is openly, broadly acknowledged. There have been great battles won and lost in its name. First in feelings, last spoken. Love—the core of being!

With the dawning of each morning
I awake amid sighs and smiles
Thinking how much I adore you
How every moment's worthwhile

Rising amid sunbeams or teardrops
Melodies stir within my heart
Reviving songs of togetherness
Definitely when we're apart

In times of minor differences
Okays override any nays
Such as life's phases come and go
We keep happy most of the days

A gaze outside the window
Catches sight of misty rain
With little sun to be seen
Just grayness, overtly plain

Toward the distant horizon
Gray skies disclose bits of blue
Rose-colored rays of sunshine
Glow for the love of you

I place a rose on your pillow
A symbol of my love for you
Each petal with special meaning
Exclusively from me to you

A smile, a giggle
A touch, a tickle—
Rhapsody in motion
Curves like a sickle

You are the bright smile
Lightening my heart
Inspiring, loving
'Til death do us part

Today, tomorrow
Let us never forget
Walks in the meadow
Or showers soaking wet

For those are the times
The very finest of them all
Ventures with Mother Nature
No matter how large or how small

If Only . . .

How often do you say "if only"? Life is better reflecting upon good days, rather than if only. See what you want to see, listen to what you want to hear, embrace all that you love! Change if only into I saw . . . I listened . . . I embraced!

If only . . .

I had one more day
To do the things I didn't do
To see the things I didn't see
To walk beneath skies of blue

If only . . .

Just one more hour to hear life's songs
To bathe in each tranquil tune
Listening with an open heart
Nighttime, morning, afternoon

If only . . .

One more minute to be so near
To touch, to feel, to caress
Mindful of lifetime's majesty
Sense nature's true openness

If only . . .

There had been more time
To savor life to its fullest

Watching intently
For the tiniest, the newest

I saw . . .

I had more time—a single day
One more hour, just one more minute
What a treasure that time is now
To rise early, to begin it

I listened . . .

And took all the necessary time
To soulfully capture each heartbeat
Storing it in the mind's scrapbook
Amidst the bitter and semisweet

I embraced . . .

More time being dedicated
To see, listen, feel each minute
Welcoming momentary time
To LIVE, to joyfully end it

Isn't it nice . . .

To have one more day
To enjoy each hour, each minute
To now find the time
To see, to do all that's in it?

Remembering . . .

Remembering a grandma brings to mind thin, wrinkled hands with a soft, caring touch and smiles of pure sunshine. Granddad exposes tired hands, muscular arms for tight hugs, never rough. Life overflows with memories.

Life is full of ageless memories
Some beloved, others buried
None without a story to tell
Numerous restful, many wearied

From loving, caring relationships
The thread of life is securely woven
Connecting happiness with sorrow
Inside events totally unchosen

Family separations
Make members feel worlds apart
Hope heals lonely bitterness
Filling emptiness of heart

Friends, loved ones departed
Leave spirits whispering within
To be good examples
As you begin to live again

With each day that steadily passes
A page of life's diary is turning
Since life's overflowing with memories
You must forever be remembering . . .

What surprises have frequently tempted you in nature? Soft breezes whisper to the trees as the dragonfly lifts vertically. Do you see it? The hummingbird's tail whistles. Do you hear it? A rippling stream evokes a sense of calm. Do you feel it? Mother Nature's presence touches your heart while you experience peace within your soul. Sense the tranquility. Walk with mindfulness attuned to the miraculous choreography of Earth's symphony.

Presence of Spirit

Do you hold nature's spirit at the center of your being?

SPIRIT OF NATURE

Nature touched me, kissed my hand
Dragonfly wings helped me understand
So much spirit in wildlife to see
Long-lasting essence before me

Flora struggles within a rocky bed
Deer in a dense forest forge ahead
Life's bravery stands triumphantly
As I express my own soliloquy

Nature's Spirit—
It's compelling. It's foretelling.
It's profound. It's all around.

Thought for a New Day: *By loving, life becomes more enjoyable in the moments, with each one a special treasure. Focus on the love!*

THREAD OF LIFE

An opportunity for a second chance is a gift. Right a wrong, start over, mend a broken heart, ask for forgiveness, or forgive. When a change in life comes, Mother Nature's spirit helps guide the way. Seek comfort where time slows, binding the heart with nature.

Life's trials weave as a winding road
Amid twists and turns that abound
End to a somewhat bottomless pit
Stretches within sight, without sound

Existence shrouded in shades of gray
Leaves deep thought welling emotions
Nourishment through faith sustains hope
Shortens mountains, recedes oceans

Part of life's thread remains unbroken
That which binds heart with the mind
Righting a wrong, beginning anew
A second chance is a humbling find

Peaceful, listening, thankful traits
Straighten weaves of the winding road
Time finds a way to come back around
With ventures of nature's obvious code

Peace in the hills, quiet of still waters
Cast changed views as new life has begun
What once was understood as forsaken
Becomes a challenge, a fight to be won!

Voyages: Life's Journeys

Journeys along the rivers of life present choices to be made. Much akin to rivers flowing downstream, life glides with ease. Then, days pass, flowing against the current, tumbling over rocky beds. Within those times of hardship, you find a renewed spirit toward triumph.

From the moment of birth
Resolute destiny is set
To travel life's journeys
Overcoming fear, no regret

Outside is waiting, calling
To see what you can see
Perseverance is stalwart
To be what you can be

From a desert oasis
To a sun-drenched island
Warm amazing adventures
Surround like a garland

Flowers of the fields
Covering land like the dew
Could be choking weeds
Or blossoms fresh, anew

Rivers meander, twist and turn
Along paths Mother Nature treads
Much like your journeys of life
Cascading over rocky beds

One day may be somber
The next, glad instead
As each new path of life
Reaches far ahead

Voyages from year to year
Touch varying walks of life
Those of understanding
Many of emotional strife

Storms come, storms go
On the edge of fears
Forgiveness heals
Cleansed with nature's tears

Pages of life's scrapbook
Might be ragged, may be torn
Filled with worn images
Of the lost, lonely, forlorn

Chapters once rewritten
Instill ways to understand
Journeys across life's paths
Reach out with a helping hand

AGING GRACEFULLY

No one enjoys the effects of growing old, but no one seeks the alternative either. You cannot control how fast or slow the sands of the hourglass fall. Change your mindset toward aging, accept each shift with grace.

In the beginning . . .

When you were young
Your whole life lay ahead
Visions of bliss
Overruled any dread

Never thought about aging
No need for worry
Believed youth everlasting
Pure joy, more flurry

Walked along velvety paths
Happy as could be
Frolicked with Mother Nature
Life was so carefree

Then, one day . . .

You looked in the mirror
Stunned at what you saw
Tired, aging too fast
Noting every flaw

One day to the next
Uncertainty appeared

Handling life's challenges
Something to be revered

From now on . . .

As the days dwindle down
Toward ending the year
Life takes on new meaning
More joy, less and less fear

As each year passes
Accept every wrinkle
Let lines in life's diary
Smile with a twinkle

After all . . .

Life is how it's played
Each day graciously
One day at a time
Aging gracefully

Focus on moments
Rather than days
Cherish memories
Within each phase

Walk along velvety paths
Happy as can be
Frolic with Mother Nature
Make life carefree

Life Begins, Life Ends

What you do with your time—days, weeks, months, years—matters. Within every day, life narrows to minutes, often seconds, which produce valued moments. Inside each esteemed moment lies the framework of your life's legacy.

Daily overarching question
"When am I going to die?"
Dangles in life's balance
As you observe time fly

Is an answer truly sought?
Perhaps thoughts of death you fear
Are sights slight, oftentimes cloudy
Or visions strong, perfectly clear?

What lives, surely dies
Trees, birds, butterflies, flowers
Each life span differs
Merely minutes, maybe hours

Some given only a morning
Others last 'til afternoon
Beauty too quickly vanishes
Leaving nature all too soon

Earthly life—what a priceless gift!
Treasured in every way
Noteworthy and valued
Moment by moment, day by day

Does it sincerely matter?
The month, day, year, or time
No! How you live matters
Superlative to sublime

No doubt you are going to die
Life slips away second by second
Like sand falling through an hourglass
Each lone grain to faithfully reckon

Ensure your time clock
Ticks wildly void of darkness
With an ever-pleasing sound
Grounded in gladness

Walk among the wildflowers
Wade with the tadpoles in a stream
Enjoy life's many blessings
In reality, like a dream

Highways & Byways

Roads of travel can be long and winding, straight and narrow, heavily traveled, or seldom used. Crossroads occur with dead-ends or changes in course. The same goes for life where highways and byways twist, turn, parallel, cross, stop, or continue until done.

Tales to be told, songs to be sung
Ride life's buses, subways, and rails
Memories stored in hearts, in minds
Traverse muddy swamp roads and trails

Buried in the deep shadows of the mind
Stories relate to happiness, to grief
Some mirror dispiritedness, coldness
Others parallel faith with firm belief

Numerous detours along the way
Emulate diversions, twirls, twists, turns
Crossroad moments frequently occur
Forestalling any desire that burns

Living, laughing, loving, longing
Endure with no time to borrow
Paths of pain, loneliness remain
Yesterday, today, tomorrow

Dust of the common highway
A peaceful mind quickly declines
Life ebbs of laughter, of love
As Mother Nature intertwines

Have you at some point in time sought the right words to tender an emotion, offer inspiration, or purpose newfound knowledge? In future searches, awaken your senses to the world around you. Today, more than ever, remain thankful for the beauty of this Earth that brings abundant gratefulness for simply being alive. The wonders of Mother Nature go beyond imagination capturing priceless moments each morning as you awaken in anticipation.

Awakening

Have you discovered what you might be missing?

FIXIN' WHAT'S MISSIN'

What if you missed that falling star
Or catching a lightning bug in a jar?
Missed winter turning into spring
Or any of nature's wondrous things?

Watch the falling star, make a wish
Catch the lightning bug in a dish
Witness nature's seasonal changes
Prairie grasses to mountain ranges

Fixin' what's missin'—
It's perceiving. It's believing.
It's knowing. It's growing.

Thought for a New Day: *Discover your passions, nurture your inner self, for only when you savor it, can transformation begin. Propose new awakenings!*

~ Thrill of a New Sun! ~

A new sun begins its journey across the sky. You awake to scattered thoughts before both feet hit the floor. Some flutter with ease like butterfly wings. Others sting as a painful flame after fighting dragons all night.

Daily events, good and bad, reflect both, along with a few butterfly dragons. Life offers choices. Smell the freshness of the outdoors. Feel the warmth of the sun. Listen to dawn's chorus as it begins right before sunrise.

You can turn yourself on or tune yourself out!
You can flutter with the butterflies or fly with the dragons.

ENJOY THE THRILL!

Catnip offers times to observe, listen, embrace, breathe, and savor life as you walk with Mother Nature. Observe the little things, listen for new songs, embrace the moments. Go forth with renewed breath and enjoy the thrill of it all!

Time to get up sleepy head!
Much to be discovered, explored
Inspiration awaits this day
No butterflies or dragons ignored

Rise up full force ahead
Look for splendor unseen
Relish sights with candor
Everything in between

Open a window
Absorb all that you see
Listen intently
Alert as you can be

Step outside your door
Welcome each sunray
Breathe deeply with ease
Treasure the new day

*Observe life at its best
Listen to life's songs*
Notice each little thing
Which truly belongs

Embrace life's bounties
Outside of daily strife
Enjoy the surroundings
Breathe the breath of life

As soon as the rooster crows
Rise promptly for he persists
Answer Mother Nature's call
Savor life to its fullest!

Experience Life! *Go forth. Enjoy the thrill!*

There is not one blade of grass, there is no color in this world that is not intended to make us rejoice.
— John Calvin (Theologian, 1509–1564)

WHY CATNIP

Catnip: *an intense attraction that excites or mellows a state of mind or emotion*

Mother Nature is intense, yet offers tranquil moments to soothe and heal. Reflective of the effects catnip has on the cat, the marvels of nature *excite or mellow a state of mind or emotion*. The natural world is a place of wonder and mystery where the catnip of life thrives. Whether a brilliant sunrise, an explosive sunset, amber waves of grain, or a meadow blooming with wildflowers, Mother Nature electrifies or softens the atmosphere.

— *Catnip of Life*

Epilogue

> To lift your spirits, spend time with nature. She will lend you her power until you become aware of your own.
> — Erika Nortemann

Are you aware cats love to nap in a basket? Place one in a hideaway or nook and see how long it stays empty. It is a cat magnet—with or without the sprinkle of catnip. The touch of the basket offers a sense of security, making a catnap safe and cozy.

Within Catnip's pages, many threads crisscross, comparative to the weave of a basket. Same as life, the basket is fragile. When one strand breaks, a scar of wear and tear is visible. Thus, it weakens the durability.

A common thread weaves its way through Catnip's words—*nature*. It takes little effort to discover what is right in front of you. Nature excites and bites. While life-giving and nurturing, be aware of Mother Nature's moodiness. Remember the cat.

Mother Nature is ever-present, and her moods, as with the cat, can change within a moment's notice. Nature is fragile, same as the basket, with scars defining moments long remembered. Be mindful of life's songs of strength and perseverance.

Open nature's doorway, inhale with a deep breath, exhale with a sigh, and take Mother Nature by the hand. Enjoy restful moments that still the mind and soothe the soul. With a newfound awareness, listen to the whisperings that surround you and expect the unexpected. Note what's been there but gone unnoticed—*until now!*

Observe life at its best, Listen to life's songs,
Embrace life's bounties, Breathe the breath of life,
Savor life to its fullest!

The End . . . YOUR Beginning!

Store visions of the *Catnip of Life* in your mind's diary. Visit often. Nature's enchantment awaits your walk in Mother Nature's footsteps. Whether sunlit days, moonlit nights, or in the midst of stormy weather, be present in the moment of renewal.

Seek daily contact with Mother Nature to revitalize your spirit!
— Catnip of Life

ABOUT THE AUTHOR

Sharla Lee (Shults) fulfilled her childhood desire to become an educator, graduating from Troy University in Alabama. Upon graduation, she began teaching high school chemistry and mathematics in Alabama, then a move to Ohio led her to the middle school classroom. After four years, she ventured outside education and began a second career in the railroad industry.

Sharla reentered the educational field after an eleven-year break, and her experiences from her railroad career provided a real-world connection to the classroom. She worked with Special Olympics and was instrumental in establishing Exchange Club youth organizations in three high schools located in Panama City, Florida. Sharla's last year in the classroom involved working with teens in an at-risk dropout prevention program. While involved in this endeavor, she introduced a Poetic Math Challenge, which uncovered her passion as a poetic mathematician and a new formula for success.

In 2001, Sharla once again left the classroom but remained in the field of education with Beacon Educator in the Bay District

School System, writing curriculum and providing professional development for teachers across the state of Florida. She semi-retired in 2008, at which time she became an Online Learning Specialist for Beacon.

Her previous books include *Echoes (2004)*, *Remembering (2009)*, and *Awakenings (2012)*. Upcoming books include *A Touch of Catnip*, *Voices in Nature*, and *Buzzin'*, a children's title.

Sharla resides in Florida with her calico Norwegian Forest cat, Foxie. She enjoys playing golf, listening to music, and walking in nature. Her most enjoyable moments are spent with family and grandchildren, in which she gathers inspiration for her next writing ventures.

www.ingramcontent.com/pod-product-compliance
Lightning Source LLC
Chambersburg PA
CBHW071154160426
43196CB00011B/2083